# HOME SERVICE EMPIRE

## HOW I BUILT, SCALED, AND SOLD A FAMILY OF BUSINESSES WORTH OVER $100 MILLION

### CAMERON BAWDEN

WITH CLAY MANLEY

ISBN: 978-1-968339-86-9 (ebook)

ISBN: 978-1-968339-85-2 (paperback)

ISBN: 978-1-968339-84-5 (hardcover)

For more information about Cameron Bawden, scan the QR code below:

"I've watched Cameron set bold goals his entire life—from leading on the basketball court to earning his pilot's license in high school—and what's always stood out to me is his relentless follow-through. He doesn't just dream big; he does the work. Cameron has never settled for average in anything he pursues, and as his mother, I couldn't be more proud of the man he's become. His discipline and drive are why I've always known he would be successful. If you want to learn from someone who leads by example and truly lives what he teaches, this book is for you."

—Audrey Ryan, Cameron's momma

"Cameron is one of the most dedicated and hardworking people I know; anyone who works with him quickly sees how much passion and integrity he brings to everything he does—and you will too through this book."

—Kayla Snyder, Cameron's former executive assistant

"I've known Cameron most of his adult life and watched him succeed in every area that matters: family, friends, health, work, and faith. This book is the next best thing to having him as a friend and mentor by your side."

—Rob Horne, former CEO, Drylux Restoration

"As my mentor, friend, and business partner for eight years, Cameron has been instrumental in my entrepreneurial journey —I call him the Kobe Bryant of service businesses for his unmatched work ethic, unwavering commitment, and winning mindset. I have no doubt the invaluable insights and proven strategies packed inside this book will guide you and your venture to the next level, too."

—Evan Ritchey, Cameron's business partner

"When Cameron first pitched me on Green Mango Pest Control, he didn't just ask for funding—he declared a vision: 'Dad, we're going to build the largest privately held pest control company in Arizona.' I believed him, because I knew the foundation he was standing on.

From day one, Cameron built his company around timeless principles—be your word, take full responsibility, lead with integrity, and treat people right. Those weren't slogans to him; they were the standards he lived by. Watching him take those ideas, scale them, and turn them into a company that became an industry leader has been one of the great privileges of my life to be a part of. Who Cameron became through the process was the most gratifying as his father.

What Cameron shares in *Home Service Empire* isn't theory—it's a proven blueprint for how values, systems, and belief can create extraordinary results. I've seen firsthand how he built a culture of excellence that transformed people, not just profits.

If you're serious about building a business that lasts—and becoming the kind of leader people want to follow—read this book carefully. It's written by someone who didn't just talk about success; he lived it, built it, and inspired others to do the same."

—Clyde Bawden, angel investor, mentor, and Cameron's father


"I'm grateful for the honesty and knowledge Cam poured into this book for others to learn from. I love seeing how fulfilled he is when he helps a young entrepreneur grow their business or when someone comes up just to introduce themselves and connect.

That's why reading this book has me emotional. It truly captures our ride, as every page brings back so many moments from our life together—some so good they don't feel real, and some I'd honestly rather forget.

Cam has never taken no for an answer, and this book is a reflection of just how resilient he's become. We really did start out 'young, dumb, and broke,' and yet God has blessed us with an amazing life. This whole journey with Cam, as you'll see, has been wild in the best way."

—Lyss Bawden, Cameron's wife and partner in everything

*To Banks and Ivory, so you know what it took and why we did it.*

# CONTENTS

# FOREWORD

BY TOMMY MELLO, FOUNDER OF A1 GARAGE
DOOR SERVICE

I recognized how Cameron stood out the moment I met him. Most entrepreneurs of his caliber—at least those in the home service industry—are practically overflowing with ideas without the means or the know-how to follow through or make their ideas actionable. But Cameron is different. When he and I get together, he is always in pure learning mode. He's a sponge, absorbing everything I have to offer—willing to hear feedback, asking the right questions, unafraid of failing and most importantly, implementing what he learns.

Right away, I remember telling him, "You need to double down on your personal brand, start a podcast, and write a book." Instead of pushing back or simply pretending to agree, he took notes. He internalized what I shared and started executing immediately. That's rare in this business. But that's Cameron.

What strikes me most about Cameron is his humility. He's an ambitious guy in the same industry, both of us serving similarly as leaders in our respective areas. But rather than seeing me as competition, he approached our relationship with genuine curiosity and openness to learn. He has the wisdom to know that there is room for both of us to succeed, and that my winning or finding success a bit before he did never meant he was losing or behind.

I gave him the blueprint for my success. I told him directly, "Duplicate everything we've done at A1. It took a long time to build what we have, so you can benefit from the mistakes I made and you won't have to make them yourself." Once he's equipped with the knowledge, he moves forward, full-steam ahead.

Like most entrepreneurs I know, Cameron didn't avoid the trap of thinking he could do everything at once. When he got started, he tried to build an entire ecosystem of home services: windshield repair, carpet cleaning, you name it. He had creative business names with every fruit imaginable: pineapple, coconut, varieties of all stripes. But he thankfully realized early on that he needed to narrow his focus. "Man, I'd better really go with Green Mango," he told me, once he was locked in and ready to apply what he'd learned.

And that's precisely when everything changed. He stopped trying to take all of his projects on at once and started to ruthlessly prioritize. What Cameron did with Green Mango is remarkable. He built his pest control business using strategies I've never thought of using before. While I focused on helping him with digital marketing and the company's Google presence, he was crushing it with radio spots and affiliate marketing. He had an innate ability to use influencer marketing before most of us realized what that meant for a business's online presence. He designed cool shirts that I still wear because they're that good. Green Mango became so much more than a creative business name—it became a formidable brand.

I almost bought part of Green Mango at one point. Cameron and I spent a lot of time working through the details, but ultimately, it wasn't the right fit for either of us. Business deals are hard, and you need something like a prenuptial agreement for when things don't work out—because most of the time, they don't.

After our deal fell through, Cameron asked me something that really stuck with me: "Would you still be my friend?" That moment told me everything I needed to know about Cameron's character and the type of people he'd been dealing with. He explained that everyone else who had wanted to be involved, when their deals didn't work out, just stopped talking to him. They also didn't help him anymore.

I looked at him and said, "I don't care about the deal not working out. There might be a good opportunity for us to work together in the future, but if not, I'm totally fine being bros."

When Cameron sold Green Mango for tens of millions of dollars, he joined a club that not many people can access, let alone understand. Exits can be tricky for people to make the transition, but I knew he'd be fine; he's a builder like I am. We can't just sit there and bask in success. We want to build, always. That's exactly what Cameron is doing now. He's investing in different things, coaching his kids, working on Coconut (his carpet cleaning company), and figuring out his next major move.

The pest control industry gave Cameron his first major win, but it won't be his last. He has that rare combination of vision, execution, humility, and character that creates lasting success. He's learned how to prioritize, how to delegate effectively, and how to maintain relationships even when business deals don't work out.

In these pages, you're going to learn from someone who's been in the trenches, made the mistakes, learned the lessons, and come out stronger. Cameron's not just sharing a theory—he's sharing battle-tested strategies as someone who's built something real and significant.

Pay attention. Implement what resonates. And remember: perfection is the enemy of doing good—of doing work worth doing.

*Tommy Mello is the founder of A1 Garage Door Service and the author of multiple business books. He has built his company to over 900 employees and helps other entrepreneurs scale their home service businesses.*

Cameron and A1 Founder Tommy Mello hugging

# INTRODUCTION

On May 25, 1978, legendary fighter pilot Bob Hoover faced a death sentence. Just after takeoff from San Diego's Brown Field, both of his plane's engines failed...at the same time. With two passengers aboard, the aircraft plunged into freefall.

Hoover managed to stabilize the powerless plane and, miraculously, land it in a rugged ravine. Even more astonishing, he and both passengers walked away without a scratch. Grateful to be alive, Hoover immediately ran a mental autopsy of the incident, asking himself the first and only question any responsible pilot would:

Why?

At first glance, everything checked out. Manifold pressure: normal. RPMs: steady. Fuel and oil pressure: both in the green. The gauges showed nothing wrong. And yet, the engines were dead, Hoover's knuckles were white, and his passengers had just watched their lives flash before their eyes.

The renowned pilot rushed to the side of the aircraft and whipped open the fuel drain valve. He took a long whiff.

*Bingo.*

The scent of jet fuel filled the air. He had his answer.

The plane's engines failed because a mechanic had filled the tanks with jet fuel instead of aviation gasoline. It was like filling a Formula 1 car with cooking oil—the wrong fuel for the job.

When Hoover returned to the airfield, he found the mechanic responsible. The young man stood frozen, tears streaming down his face as the pilot approached, no doubt expecting the worst.

But what happened next was extraordinary. Instead of exploding in anger, Hoover wrapped his arm around the ashamed mechanic and, according to the *California Fullerton News-Tribune*, said, "There isn't a man alive who hasn't made a mistake. But I'm positive you'll never make this mistake again. That's why," Hoover continued, "I want to make sure that you're the only one to refuel my plane tomorrow. I won't let anyone else on the field touch it."

*Wow.*

I'm no Bob Hoover, but we share two things in common:

1.  A deep love for aviation. Mine was passed down to me from my father.
2.  A belief that mistakes are life's most valuable teachers.

The Wright brothers would agree.

Over several years, they tested their designs tirelessly. They flew whenever conditions allowed, failing often but learning with each attempt. Their method was simple: test, observe, adjust, and try again. It was about progress, not perfection. *Ready, fire, aim,* as I like to say. By learning from their mistakes, they accomplished the impossible.

That same opportunity is in front of you.

Over 14 years in business, I made millions of dollars' worth of avoidable mistakes. It was nearly a decade and a half of trial and error with my primary business, Green Mango Pest Control, as well as other service businesses I started. Eventually, I accomplished what once felt impossible: guiding a company I built from scratch to a near nine-figure acquisition—and exiting entirely on my terms.

Learning from mistakes worked for me. It worked for Bob Hoover. It worked for the Wright brothers. And it can absolutely work for you, too.

As George Bernard Shaw said, "Success does not consist in never making mistakes, but in never making the same one a second time." Put another way, mistakes are like jet fuel for progress.

"I don't think I possess any skill that anyone else doesn't have," Bob Hoover later reflected. "I've just had perhaps more of an opportunity, more of an exposure, and been fortunate to survive a lot of situations that many others weren't so lucky to make it."

Survival: That's entrepreneurship in a nutshell. It's not about avoiding mistakes; it's about embracing them, learning from them, and surviving long enough to make them work in your favor.

This book is your chance to learn from my most brutal mess-ups without going through the pain yourself. I made the mistakes so you don't have to.

My goal is to help you avoid the setbacks, speed up your progress, and accomplish more than you ever thought possible. When that happens, we both win.

*Ready. Fire. Aim.*

ONE

MY STORY



"We're done," I muttered, sneezing into the stifling
desert air.

The backyard felt like an oven. Ankle-high weeds tangled
around my shoes like shackles. The desert sun scorched my
stinging eyes until I could barely see straight. The stench of dog
poop clung to everything—my equipment, my clothes, my skin.
Even after I left this house, I knew the smell would follow, a
lingering reminder of everything I couldn't seem to escape.

This wasn't just another bad day. This was the day I realized the business I'd poured everything into was broken...and
so was I.

After three long years of knocking on strangers' doors
across the Valley, I was still landing bottom-tier accounts, still
spraying pest-infested yards myself, still trudging through the

same sun-scorched neighborhoods I'd started in, and still watching doors slam in my face.

While most kids my age were tossing graduation caps, locking down job offers with steady paychecks, 401(k)s, and central air, or prepping for their next steps as doctors, lawyers, and engineers, all my hard work had led me here: melting into the dirt of a Maricopa backyard, reeking of dog crap and disappointment...as the neighborhood bug man.

Choking back another sneeze, I couldn't help but think that this wasn't what I'd pictured when I set out to build an empire.

Back then, I had big dreams. "We're going to build the biggest pest control company in Arizona," I'd promised, blinded by ambition and the kind of naive confidence that only comes when you have no clue what you're doing (or what you're in for).

Now?

All I wanted was out. Out of the backyard, out of the business, out of the debt, and out of this mess I'd dragged my family into.

"Ah-choo!" Another sneeze rattled my chest.

"You can't make money in pest control," I confessed, my voice shaking under the weight of frustration and defeat. I wasn't sure if I was trying to convince my father on the other end of the line or myself.

As I wiped my leaking nose with my sleeve, the absurdity hit me: I'd built my life around a product I was allergic to. The perfect metaphor, I thought, for a business that seemed determined to choke the life out of me.

And at that moment, it nearly had.

Dad stayed silent. He didn't need to say anything. I owed him everything—the seed money, the belief, the patience. Sadly, he'd lost everything once before, and I knew it. What if I was the reason my dad, of all people, had to suffer all over *again*?

All I wanted was to pay him back and walk away.

Dusty, my business partner, was on the call too. He was just as broke, just as beaten down, and just as ready to walk away. For years, we'd worn every hat just to keep the lights on. We were salesmen, techs, accountants, secretaries, janitors, marketers, even amateur models. We had no idea what we were doing, but if it needed doing, we did it.

And still, it wasn't enough. Every ounce of energy, every sliver of hope, every shred of self-confidence we'd started with was melting away beneath the punishing Arizona sun.

I'd even pulled my wife, Lyss, and our newborn son, Banks, into the whole ordeal.

Lyss believed in me when no one else would, willingly moving into a motor home to minimize our expenses *and* working one, two, then basically three jobs to help us make ends meet. First she taught dance lessons. Then she took a job at an endodontist's office. Her third gig? Pest control—as a volunteer, of course. (The business couldn't afford to pay either one of us.)

It wasn't unusual for her to work around the clock, just so I could do the same chasing a future that felt like a dead end.

One afternoon, she strapped on rollerblades, stuffed her vest with thirty pounds of flyers, and hit the streets to spread the word. At barely 100 pounds, she looked like a petite Michelin Man on skates, wobbling under the weight of it all. Then, boom. She faceplanted, eating hard, unforgiving concrete.

I couldn't stop picturing her sprawled out on the pavement for a business that couldn't offer her anything, yet she never once complained. At that point, we were all eating concrete: Lyss, Dusty, my dad, and me.

I felt responsible for all of it.

Worst of all, even though Banks didn't know it yet, I'd promised him a better future, too. Now I had no idea how to keep that promise.

That morning in Maricopa, we decided to sell the business for whatever we could get as long as it meant paying my dad back. Dusty and I would likely walk away with nothing. My dad's return would almost certainly be a flat zero. It might go down as the worst investment he ever made. At that point, even selling for pennies on the dollar felt worth it if it meant escaping the crushing pressure of gambling his savings, our relationship, Lyss's health, our marriage, my sanity, and my son's future on a business that couldn't pay any of us while it slowly drained the life out of all of us.

The good news was I had every reason to believe there would be a buyer.

I learned early on that service businesses are surprisingly attractive to buyers, thanks to my first entrepreneurial endeavor, On the Spot. (I'd ask if you've heard of it, but I can almost guarantee you haven't.)

On the Spot trailer

About a year before launching Green Mango, I sank what little money I had—money that could've easily gone to college tuition—into a beat-up trailer and a power washer. My "business plan" was simple: wash and detail cars, on the spot. It wasn't much, but it was mine.

Who knew it'd be my first of seven service businesses?

Maybe you've had a similar start: lemonade stands, mowing lawns, washing cars, selling candy bars at a markup, or coaching Little Leaguers. Anything to earn a few bucks and get a taste of what it's like to build something from nothing. Whatever it was, you know the feeling of trying to turn a little into a lot, and the lessons that come with it. For me, the biggest lesson was this: There's always a buyer...or so I thought.

A few months later, I sold On the Spot on Craigslist for something like 10,000 bucks. A portion went to the best investment I ever made: a wedding ring for Lyss. The rest went straight into a spray rig for my truck, thanks to the best salesman I know: Dusty.

First, Dusty sold me on being his business partner. Then he sold me on the dumbest name ever: Green Mango Pest Control. Like me, Dusty had gone on a two-year church mission. Mine was in Canada, while his was in Brazil, where mangos were basically a food group.

"Green Mango will be our way of life. It's how we'll eat," he explained, hence the Mango. As for the Green part, that was our nod to "cleaning up" the pest control industry with organic products that were safe for pets and people.

We each brought a truck to the table. Mine had airbags; his didn't. When we weren't out hunting for customers or spraying their homes, we worked from our "office." My mom ran her business downstairs, doing nails for clients as if the kitchen were a salon. Dusty and I were upstairs, running ours from my bedroom. We had a desktop computer, a rinky-dink flip phone, and a closet.

My first truck

No joke, the closet might've been our most valuable asset. After two years of getting doors slammed in my face in Canada, I came home with skin thick enough to try door-to-door sales. Like most home service businesses, we started by knocking on strangers' doors, pitching pest control to anyone who'd listen. We'd knock neighborhoods well into the evening, then I'd knock on my closet door all night. Dusty would crack it open, playing the skeptical homeowner. We role-played for hours, practicing until my pitch was as airtight as his.

Our business model was sell, spray, reinvest, repeat. We wrapped both trucks with our logo and parked them in all the right places. Just one month into Green Mango, when Lyss and I got married, Dusty parked one of the trucks right outside our wedding. "Free advertising," he said with a shrug. Sweat equity and free advertising. That's what got us off the ground.

With On the Spot, I'd proven I could build something and sell it. But Green Mango wasn't On the Spot. Three years later, no legitimate buyer would touch it with a 10-foot pole.

As 2013 came to a close, we were at rock bottom—broke, exhausted, and convinced we'd hit a dead end. Dusty and I were running on fumes. So was Lyss, especially now with Banks in the mix. We couldn't imagine spending another day knocking on more doors, spraying more yards, and wondering when we'd ever be able to afford to pay someone else to do it, let alone pay ourselves. But what choice did we have? Without a buyer, there was no way out.

Shortly after that morning in Maricopa, three full years into our Green Mango journey, the cruel reality hit me: We were trapped.

And somehow, that ended up being one of the best things that ever happened to me.

I made every mistake in the book on my 11-year journey from that desperate morning in Maricopa to my exit—but I survived to tell the story.

I came face-to-face with a team of federal agents. I felt the phantom heart pangs of overwork, pain so real I paid for cardiac tests out of pocket just to make sure I wasn't about to drop dead at 35. I packed on 30 pounds until I barely recognized the man in the mirror. I missed bedtimes and ballgames. I fired friends I loved and family I couldn't imagine losing.

Even when I made the right calls, I had to constantly remind myself that I was still a good guy. Doing the right thing, I learned, doesn't always feel good.

While Green Mango was still growing, I launched five additional service businesses. Each one ushered in its own set of pressures. Despite my best efforts, three of them flamed out fast, either shutting down or selling for pennies on the dollar.

That all falls under what I call the unquantifiable pressures of entrepreneurship: pressures that no founder is immune to, especially a guy with no experience, no formal education, and nothing particularly special about him.

Of course, there were quantifiable pressures too.

At one point, I woke up $4 million in debt. When everyone else thought I was winning, I was floating payroll with my own money, down to the last $1.88 in my account. Eventually, I bought out Dusty, betting millions on myself that I couldn't afford to lose.

Despite all that, I feel like the most blessed man in the world. My life today feels surreal, even to me.

So don't feel bad for me. This is all completely normal. It's textbook stuff. It's entrepreneurship. It's not for the faint of heart. It's not supposed to be.

While others glorify the grind, I'd rather you know what you're really in for. Think of your entrepreneurial journey like a video game: The bosses only get bigger and badder the further you go. Every new level of success requires a correspondingly deeper level of sacrifice, which is exactly why so many entrepreneurs give up at the same time that we were desperately searching for a buyer.

My goal is to guide you further than ever before.

You see, in our first handful of years, we were just building to survive. We didn't have a real plan, let alone a system. We had the trucks, the closet, and the flip phone. That was it.

Eventually, we started building to grow. We added more vehicles, more customers, more employees, and even a real customer relationship management system (CRM) to track it all. Yet we were still just inching forward without clear direction. It wasn't until much later that we made the final shift that changed everything: We started building to sell.

If I'd known what I know now, we would have built to sell from day one.

By the time I exited, Green Mango was generating $27 million in annual revenue with whopping 30 percent-plus profit margins. We'd become the largest privately owned pest control company in Arizona.

To put that into perspective, it's been said only four percent of businesses surpass $1 million in annual revenue. And of that four percent, only about seven percent reach $10 million.

That means as few as 0.3 percent ever get there—and even fewer do it profitably. In other words, we joined the 1% Club.

By 2024, my eyes turned to saucers as escalating offers came pouring in: $40 million, then $50 million, then $60 million, all for that locally owned and operated pest control business I started with a buddy.

And somehow, I said no to all of them.

Then on October 2, 2024, after 14 years in the game, I officially closed on an offer I couldn't refuse, pulling my chips off the table for good.

Like I said, I'm so glad I didn't quit.

You see, exiting a business is rare. Exiting on your terms is rarer. I'm proud to say I did both—and now, I want to help you do the same. Given the odds, that may seem impossible, but here's why it's not: I'm just a regular guy. I grew up a rail-thin, painfully shy C student with a bad haircut. I've never completed a college course. My greatest mental triumph? Solving a Rubik's Cube...thanks to YouTube.

Love him or hate him, Elon Musk nailed it when he said, "Starting a company is like chewing glass and staring into the abyss." I'm living proof that you don't need to be an alien, a rocket scientist, or even a college graduate to succeed.

You just have to be willing to eat glass.

That willingness alone propelled us from being unsellable in 2013 to *refusing* to sell in 2016. It powered us through almost six years of doubt, sacrifice, and survival until seven-figure revenue became normal and we could finally afford to pay ourselves.

It's propelled plenty of other founders there, too.

But if you want to break beyond $1 to $3 million in annual revenue—and do it without losing your family, your health, or your sanity—you need something more than grit. You need a system.

You need a system that doesn't rely on you grinding 24/7 but instead allows your business to grow, scale, and thrive with or without you.

Because if it all falls apart without you, what are you really building?

More importantly, you need a system that makes your business so irresistible that even if you want to keep it forever, buyers will fight to take it off your hands.

That's what happened to me.

But I didn't start with a system. We built almost everything the hard way, mistake by painful mistake, over more than a decade of racking them up.

That's why I wrote this book. To give you what I never had: a proven system. A clear blueprint. A playbook to break through faster, scale smarter, and build a business buyers fight for—even if you decide to keep it forever.

Building to sell isn't just about cashing out; it's about never feeling trapped again.

The lessons I learned through the grind, the setbacks, the wins, and the losses weren't just for me. They're for anyone bold enough to build something of their own.

Building to sell gives you options. It gives you leverage. It gives you your life back. It forever changes how your business is structured, run, and valued—for the better. That means higher revenue, better margins, and more time freedom, no matter how trapped you might feel right now.

Whether you want to scale, exit, or simply create a business that works for you instead of the other way around, building to sell starts with understanding one thing: the Value Vortex.

Let's get into it.

# THE VALUE VORTEX

Famed aviator and author Antoine de Saint-Exupéry once said, "Perfection is attained not when there is nothing more to add, but when there is no longer anything to take away." The same is true for building a business that sells.

That's why the backbone of this book is the Value Vortex. It's my nine-point compass that reveals exactly what buyers value most and what matters most for you as a founder. Think of it like a wheel with just nine spokes: I stripped away the "trivial many" so you can focus on the "vital few."

These nine spokes are the 20 percent of actions that drive at least 80 percent of results. They're the compound movements of building a business that sells.

The Value Vortex is forged from real-world experience: seven businesses I built and six I scaled, five exits totaling more than $100 million, multiple franchises launched and sold across markets and states, hundreds of trainings and talks, millions of dollars in painful mistakes, and more than 60 in-depth meetings with potential buyers (private equity firms and strategic acquirers) that ultimately led to the exit of a lifetime.

A *sellable* business is a *simple* business. As you can see below, the genius of the Value Vortex lies in its simplicity.

# THE VALUE VORTEX

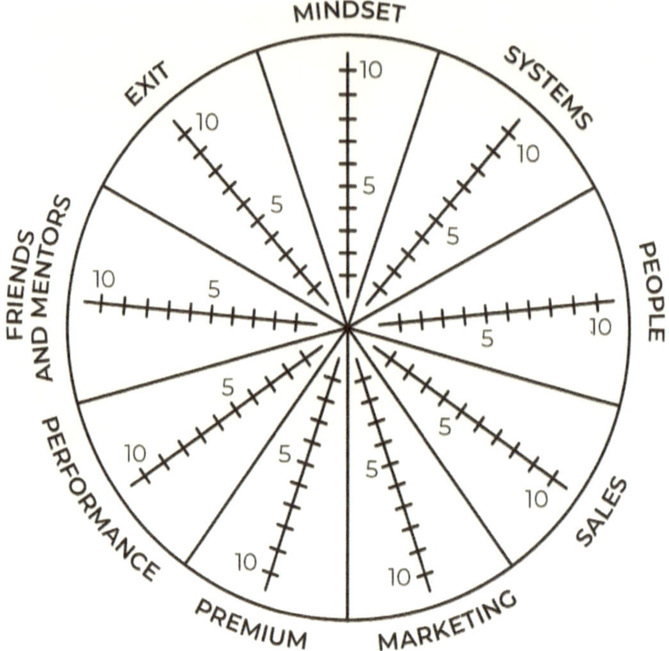


In the chapters ahead, we'll unpack each of the nine universal keys, working our way around the Vortex to equip you with my best tools, frameworks, and strategies to build, scale, and exit on your terms.

## Why It Matters

Unlike my earlier exits, which were rushed or reactive, I got everything I wanted for the first time when I sold Green

Mango: top dollar, total freedom, and the peace of mind I'd promised my family.

Without the principles in this book, Green Mango could've ended up like my more unfortunate past business ventures: Pineapple Pools, Agave Autoglass, and Black Hat Security—fire-sold, lowballed, or flat-out dead.

Because here's the truth that nobody told me: Buyers aren't sentimental. They're smart, they're trained, and they're strategic. Buyers put no value on the bits of concrete you picked from your pregnant wife's hair after she faceplanted while promoting your business. They won't increase your multiple for the nights you lay awake staring holes in the ceiling, wondering if payroll would clear. They won't reimburse you for the stress tests either. And they certainly won't factor in any of the bedtimes, ballgames, or recitals you missed along the way.

It's just business, and buyers care most about what your business is worth *without* you. So how do you build a business that serves them and you at the same time?

With the Value Vortex.

With it, you'll be equipped to attract the kind of irresistible offers that make your blood, sweat, and tears finally worth it. You'll command leverage. You'll exit on your terms. Or you'll build a business you could happily keep forever—because it works for you, not the other way around.

Either way, you win.


## How to Use the Value Vortex

Think of it like Zig Ziglar's Wheel of Life or the life balance wheel popularized by Tony Robbins. It works the same way. Your Vortex is a snapshot of where you stand and where you need to improve.

Here's how to use it:

1. **Score yourself quarterly** in each of the nine categories on a scale from 1 to 10.
2. **Plot your scores.** You'll instantly see where you're strong, where you're weak, and where to focus.
3. **Push outward.** The goal is to raise every score closer to 10. The further out you get, the more valuable, scalable, and sellable your business becomes. As a bonus, you'll feel the benefits even if you never sell.

As Tony Robbins teaches, what you focus on expands. That's exactly what you want to do: *expand* your scores. When one spoke gets stronger, the entire Vortex gets stronger. And when the Vortex gets stronger, everything expands with it—including revenue, margins, options, freedom, and value.

Even small improvements in any of these nine areas can unlock massive value. A point or two in any category could add $5 million, $10 million, or even $20 million to your bottom line or your valuation, depending on the size of your business. And what if those same improvements gave you back five, 10, even 20 hours of freedom each month (maybe even each week) after years of sacrifice? Best of all, a point or two is just the tip of the iceberg when you apply what I share in the pages ahead.

This is the tool I wish I'd had when I was starting out. In hindsight, it's the reason I was able to turn a scrappy, locally owned pest control company into a near nine-figure exit.

And now, it's yours.

But before we begin, a quick word to the wise:

*"We cannot become what we want by remaining what we are."*
—Max DePree

Before you can build a business worth millions, you must first build the person worthy of those millions.

When I was a teenager, my identity was simple: I was a kid chasing my dream of flying helicopters with my dad. Everything I did was aligned with that identity—attending ground school, logging hours, studying aviation theory. Do you think someone who identifies as a teenager, even one with a pilot's license, is equipped to build and sell a multimillion-dollar business?

Of course not.

I was more equipped to chase girls, shoot hoops, and stick my head in the clouds than build an empire. But when we launched Green Mango, I couldn't act like a kid anymore. I had to evolve into an operator. Operators hustle. They sacrifice nights and weekends. They wear every hat until the seams split. They solve every problem themselves. Forget dreaming; they execute.

My identity became the guy who gets it done. Sound familiar? You might be that guy or gal right now. That's okay...if you evolve with your business. Because operators don't sell businesses for millions. They're too busy working *in* the business to ever build one that thrives without them. They create jobs, not assets.

That's why I had to evolve once more.

I became an owner. Owners build systems. Owners build teams. Owners build machines. Owners, unlike everybody else, *exit.*

Each evolution from teenager to operator to owner began as a belief long before it showed up as an action. Each shift drove new actions, new results, and new opportunities that once seemed impossible.

Identity precedes outcome. It always has and it always will.

Everything in these pages—every system, every framework, every strategy behind my nine figures in exits—depends on you assuming the identity of an owner right now.

Not later. Not when you hit a certain revenue goal. Not when you feel "ready." (Trust me, I was never "ready.")

Today. Now. *Ready. Fire. Aim.*

If you're still thinking like an operator, you're already building a business that no one will want to buy. And if you don't start thinking like an owner, how can you possibly build something worth owning?

To build something bigger than yourself, you must first become someone bigger.

Muhammad Ali famously declared, "I am the greatest," but here's the part most people miss, straight from the champ's mouth: "I said that even before I knew I was."

When we started Green Mango, I was shy, nervous, uncertain, and inexperienced. Eventually, I learned to rewrite my identity. Every morning, I anchored my identity work in my sacred rhythms. I stepped into the ice bath, I said my prayers, then I told myself who I was becoming. "I am charismatic." "I am confident." "I am decisive." "I am resourceful." Until it wasn't a lie anymore.

Though the words have evolved, the rhythm hasn't changed. It's still as automatic to me as brushing my teeth. Updating your identity is like lifting weights. You don't get strong and then lift—you lift and then get strong.

So before we dive into the nine spokes of the Value Vortex, make the most important shift of all: Update your identity. Speak it into existence. Step into it every single day. You are now an owner, period.

Without that update, everything that follows will feel like a foreign language; it will never stick.

Decide to become the owner worthy of the empire you're about to build before you turn the page.

Now let's get into it.

# TWO
# MINDSET



My heart was in my throat.

Familiar self-doubt flooded my body like a tidal wave. John was the biggest investor in the Valley. He was my personal white whale who I had somehow managed to reel in. Now he was, in his words, "done." And if he was done, *we* were done too.

My mind raced through every worst-case scenario: the bank repossessing everything. Lyss refusing to speak to me or even look at me. Banks, our oldest, standing on a street corner with a tattered cardboard sign in one hand. Ivory, our daughter, beside him, her tiny hands gripping his other. Moose, our loyal dog, skinny and weak.

Becoming a bug man? Spraying homes? Leading a team? *Nothing* was going according to plan. And yet this was nothing new.

You see, since I was young, I had always wanted to fly.

I had a foolproof plan: Scouts. School. Sports. Aviation. One step after another, all leading to my dream of working with my dad, showing land to real estate investors from the sky.

I was going to build a life in the clouds. Who could blame me?

Imagine being a kid, looking up and spotting a helicopter slicing through the sky, knowing your dad is the one flying it. Watching him climb into the cockpit, toss on his headset, fire up the rotors, and lift off, to me, my dad was every bit as cool as an astronaut or a movie star.

I desperately wanted to be just like him when I grew up.

Some of my earliest and most treasured memories are of rolling out of bed before dawn, heading to the hangar, then soaring toward towering peaks to catch the sun gently lighting up the desert sky, alongside my hero.

Nearly every time I caught a helicopter zipping through the air, I thought, "That could be me someday." Scratch that. "That *will* be me some day."

To my delight, my dad was all for it.

At 15 years old, while my friends were nervously learning how to parallel park, I was parking airplanes after basketball practice. By 19, I'd already earned three advanced aviation ratings, so I'd be qualified to climb right into the helicopter cockpit when I returned home from my two-year church mission. This wasn't just some boyhood dream; it was my destiny.

Until it wasn't.

When I came home in 2009, fully licensed and eager to climb into the captain's seat, I couldn't.

The recession had wiped out the market. Nobody was buying land, which meant Dad's helicopter was grounded along with my dream.

Scouts, sports, school, aviation, even my mission—every

step had gone exactly to plan, until now. I felt like an athlete who trains his entire life for the pros, only to suffer a career-ending injury in the preseason. I was sidelined before I even got a chance to play.

Ironically, that's what thrust me into the world of entrepreneurship, the very place where even the best-laid plans get ripped to shreds regularly.

That's right. Green Mango was more of a detour than a dream from the very beginning. I hadn't planned on any of it. Sometimes, though, the best things in life aren't part of the plan.

After six long years of grinding—working for free, knocking on doors, spraying homes, and reinvesting every cent—we finally broke through.

It didn't happen overnight. It never does.

There were countless mornings when I'd sit in my truck, staring at houses and wondering if today would be the day we'd wave the white flag. I was legitimately hoping a buyer or backup plan would appear ever since that morning in Maricopa. But slowly, almost invisibly, things started to shift. Our service improved. Our reputation grew. Referrals began to trickle in.

Bamboo spends years growing underground before it ever even breaks the surface, silently building roots strong enough to support what comes next. That was us: years of invisible work, laying down roots even when it felt like nothing was happening.

Then when it's finally ready, bamboo explodes, shooting out of the earth and growing up to 90 feet in mere weeks after years of hiding underground.

That was Green Mango in 2016.

After years of surviving in the dirt, we finally emerged—and for the first time, our growth was visible to everyone.

Our obsessive focus on customer service started paying off through referrals that snowballed. One satisfied customer would tell two neighbors, who'd tell their friends, who would recommend us to their family. Word of mouth became our most powerful marketing tool.

We finally upgraded from scribbled notes and manual spreadsheets to a real CRM. That meant no more invoices slipping through the cracks.

We weren't the only ones knocking on doors anymore, either. We had a team, a *real* team. Sales guys were drumming up new accounts for pure commission, which meant we could afford to keep selling. With more new accounts than Dusty and I could service ourselves, we started hiring technicians one by one, too. Techs needed trucks, so we creatively secured loans to get them. (More on that later.)

To be clear though, that didn't mean we were killing it financially.

Our margins stayed tight because we had far more expenses than the average provider, like clean trucks, premium products, a one-of-a-kind scorpion-free guarantee, and crisp Nike uniforms that didn't look like we'd slept in them. These little things were how we stood out. We agreed we wouldn't budge on them, no matter the budget. We knew they made a big difference to customers, but these premium touches came at a cost.

Eventually, our fleet multiplied from two to 25 flat-black service trucks (each with working airbags). Seeing them all lined up, wrapped in the Green Mango logo, was like something straight out of a movie. It was a surreal reminder of how far we'd come since those desperate days in Maricopa.

So yeah, in 2016 we finally hit seven figures in revenue, a number that once seemed as distant as Mars. Yet after expenses, it was just enough for Dusty and me to draw our first real paychecks—six years after starting the business.

Those paychecks felt like way more than money. They were validation. Proof that more than half a decade of sacrifice and struggle wasn't for nothing.

The timing couldn't have been better because that same year, Lyss and I welcomed a beautiful baby girl named Ivory to the world. She didn't know it yet, but Green Mango would allow us to provide for her from day one in ways I couldn't have even imagined years earlier.

I guess that's the thing about business: It's not about being the smartest or the best (trust me, I'm neither). It's about sticking with it long enough to see the breakthrough. Persistence doesn't guarantee success. But quitting guarantees failure.

For the first time since that crossroads moment in Maricopa, reeking of feces and failure, I didn't feel like a total loser. I felt like we were winning; I felt like more than just the neighborhood bug man I never wanted to be. I was actually starting to feel like a *real* entrepreneur.

That breakthrough was just the beginning. For the first time, we were thinking about how big we could go instead of worrying about how we'd even make it to next month. That taste of real success in 2016 naturally invited me to dream bigger (as we entrepreneurs do).

What if Green Mango wasn't just our pest control company? What if it was the foundation for something bigger? What if it was the start of an empire?

That's when John, the Kevin O'Leary of the Valley, came into the picture. As the old saying goes, "When the student is ready, the teacher appears." Turns out, I wasn't crazy for dreaming so big. John saw what we were starting to see: This could be so much bigger than some local pest control operation. *We* could be so much bigger than bug men.

He wasn't looking to buy Green Mango, and at that point, we wouldn't have sold it to him or anyone. He wanted to back us, Dusty and me, as we built our empire.

*Gulp.*

For a kid who'd always struggled with self-confidence, I was equally terrified and excited. This was a man who didn't know me one bit, and yet he believed in me enough to put serious money on the line. A guy known to have the power to make or break entrepreneurs was choosing *us*.

That validation meant even more than any paycheck ever could.

John's vision was to expand by launching four new service businesses, all following the Green Mango playbook. For the most part, we'd offer the exact services our Green Mango customers were already clamoring for.

"You do pests, but what about pools?" they'd ask.

"Know anyone who installs security systems?"

"If you cleaned couches like you clear spiderwebs, you'd be worth a fortune."

John saw what we did. We already had a built-in customer base, and we were ready for more. With a team in place and systems starting to form at Green Mango, the business didn't need us 24/7 anymore. Those 18-hour days we'd grown used to had shrunk to 12-hour, 10-hour, and at times, just eight-hour days. Believe it or not, I was almost starting to feel lazy.

I didn't miss spraying yards and knocking on doors, but I was open to a new challenge, especially if it meant impressing John. I guess I was a *real* entrepreneur, because that entrepreneurial itch had officially taken hold, and with John's backing I could scratch it.

With him footing the bills, we could outspend competitors

to acquire new customers, dominate the market from the outset, and grow all four new businesses far faster than I alone ever did.

The risk was minimal. The upside? Incredible.

All we had to do was what we apparently did best: launch service businesses with silly names.

The only catch was, we'd launch all four of them...at once.

Thus, Pineapple Pools, Black Hat Security, Agave Auto-glass, and Coconut Cleaning were born. Launching any business is a grind, but launching four back-to-back was pure insanity. And yet I was loving every second of it. In a weird way, it took me back to the early days of Green Mango that I had grown to occasionally miss—the challenge and rush of building something from nothing. Only this time, we had real experience and someone else's money to lean on.

We went from one business to five almost overnight. Better yet, the businesses were growing almost exactly as we had planned. By early 2018, they all had hit seven figures in revenue or were well on their way. That meant all four were set to outgrow Green Mango in less than half the time.

2016 was one of the best years of my life. 2018, on the other hand, was one of the worst.

Out of nowhere, John pulled the plug with those three little words, "I am done."

Why?

I still don't know for certain. My hunch is that he felt customer acquisition costs were suddenly too high. His bubble burst; it happens. The problem was that when he bailed, he left us holding the bag. I had nearly crumbled under the pressure of my dad's initial investment in Green Mango years earlier, and John's money made Dad's look like pocket change.

I woke up $4 million in debt the next morning. Growth

mode had left us at full throttle with no way to slam on the brakes.

Dusty and I scrambled to fund the businesses ourselves, buying time to figure out what to do and paying our people by diverting every dollar we could from Green Mango. It was like robbing Peter to pay Paul. But still it wasn't enough.

My dream had become a nightmare. *Again.*

Mike Tyson said it best: "Everybody has a plan until they get punched in the face."

John delivered the knockout blow.

I'll never forget standing in front of our Pineapple Pools team, 40 sets of eyes fixed on me like relentless spotlights. I went ice cold, my voice quaked, and my hands trembled as I broke the news: We were done. We'd immediately begin searching for a buyer, and if we couldn't find one, we'd be shutting down.

The looks of disappointment, fear, and uncertainty in their faces felt like a reflection of my own. Dozens of people who'd believed in our vision, who relied on their paychecks to feed their families, now faced an uncertain future. And it was on me.

I'd basically parted ways with two businesses—Pineapple Pools and Black Hat Security—and fired two family members before the clock struck noon. Good thing my next endeavor, Phoenix Power Solutions, hadn't gotten off the ground yet. One day, I was building an empire. The next, I was knee-deep in debt and scrambling to survive, unsure if I'd even have a single business left to save.

I slumped at my desk, emotionally drained, hiding in my office, trying—and failing—to process it all. Every shred of self-confidence I'd built over the past eight years had evaporated just like that.

Then my phone lit up with a text message: "ICE is here."

A follow-up text flew in: "They want to talk."

Next thing I knew, I was face-to-face with a team of US Immigration and Customs Enforcement agents.

Our conversation went something like this:

"Are you Cameron Bawden?"

"Yes."

"Do you own Pineapple Pools?"

"Yes."

"Call your lawyers and get them down here."

*Huh?*

"We will be going through all of your records this afternoon."

Those agents set up shop in our conference room like they owned the place. Within minutes, they discovered something else of interest: I still technically owned Pineapple Pools. And Black Hat Security. And Agave Autoglass. And Coconut Cleaning. And, of course, Green Mango Pest Control.

One by one, every business was placed under audit due to sloppy administration on behalf of Pineapple Pools. Even though we weren't hiring undocumented employees, we were missing required paperwork for the documented ones. With President Trump cracking down on documentation at the time, what should've been a slap on the wrist turned into a $400,000 fine.

It felt like everything I'd spent almost a decade building was collapsing in front of me. Suddenly, I was staring down fines I couldn't afford for two businesses I was done with and two more already drowning in debt. Vendors would come calling. Employees would expect paychecks I wasn't sure I could cover. Dozens of families would curse my name. Maybe my own would, too.

To make matters worse, the one person I confided in, Mark Fournier, sounded almost *delighted* to hear about my situation.

"Cameron, I'm *so* happy this happened."

*Happy?*

"Mark..." I choked out, "my life is over."

"Cameron," he answered calmly, "everything always works out." Then he paused. "Not always the way you expect—but always."

I didn't believe him. Not one bit. Not with $4.4 million suddenly hanging over my head. How was *that* going to work out? I did know one thing, though: Giving up was not an option. It never had been.

Not quitting is what got me through the early days of Green Mango. Not quitting is what carried me through every setback, every slammed door, and every sleepless night. Not quitting was the one constant that had guided me from that morning in Maricopa to this very moment.

My persistence was the only thing that had never failed me.

Maybe I wasn't a real entrepreneur. Maybe I still was that shy, self-conscious C student or that lost kid with no plan. Maybe Green Mango's growth had been dumb luck or a total fluke. But I, Cameron Bawden, was *not* a quitter.

And since I wasn't going to quit, I had only one choice— find another way forward. That's what winners do. It's like George M. Moore Jr. said: "A winner is just a loser who tried one more time."

Winners keep going. They turn roadblocks into detours. They find another way. That's how they keep trying. That's how they win.

As Mark puts it, a roadblock says, "Stop. You're done." A detour says, "Find another way."

The best entrepreneurs aren't the smartest or the most talented. If they were, every valedictorian would be a billionaire. They're the ones who don't stop or reverse at roadblocks, who always try one more time, who always find another way.

When people ask how I built Green Mango from nothing, how I survived $4.4 million in debt, how I sold for the multiple that I did, I tell them I never stopped.

It really is that simple.

If you take only one thing from this book so far, make it that.

When you're building any business, and especially when you're building to sell, roadblocks are inevitable. The only way you'll win is if you keep going.

## LOSERS SEE ROADBLOCKS. WINNERS SEE DETOURS.

Even if you're just getting started, you've probably faced your fair share of roadblocks already, haven't you?

In pest control, you can't grow without trucks. Vehicles were our lifeblood. You couldn't just toss our power sprayers in the trunk of a Corolla if you tried. Not only were they heavy, we had them truck-mounted so we could carry (and put down) more product than any competitor.

But when we outgrew our two trucks, we couldn't get approved for bank-issued vehicle loans because we had no credit history. And two 20-something kids looking like zombies from working around the clock didn't exactly scream "safe borrowers" to the loan officer sitting across the desk. I'm sure they assumed our bloodshot eyes were from partying all night, not working all night and spraying all day.

The no's were immediate. Comically fast. So what'd we do? We left the bank, moved the truck out of view, slid off our shirts, and slipped on new ones to disguise ourselves like we were in some kind of heist movie. Then we marched right back into that same bank, hoping they wouldn't recognize us. A detour! Guess what? We got shut down again.

But we kept going.

Eventually, we managed to secure an auto loan from a friend of a friend, a private party willing to front us vehicles on brutal terms. Still, it wasn't a dead end; it was a detour. In hindsight, that detour led to a hidden opportunity. We got a chance to build the credit we didn't have, and eventually, qualify for far better terms.

But then, as our fleet really started to grow, we hit another roadblock: Our insurance company refused to renew our policy. We were primarily hiring 16- to 18-year-olds as techs, and as you might imagine, our lead-footed teenagers were racking up more fender benders than the average insurer could stomach.

That roadblock was a double whammy. You can't grow a pest control company without trucks, *and* you can't service customers without people to drive them. Once again, we had to detour just to survive.

We agreed to fish for talent in a new pond and started seeking candidates with at least five years of driving experience to meet the insurance company's conditions. They cost us a boatload more, but our new hires turned out to be better employees. They stuck around longer, our service improved, attrition plummeted, training costs nosedived, and to the insurance company's delight, our new techs were better behind the wheel too. As it turned out, that detour paid off handsomely.

Soon after, we were encouraged to install cameras in our vehicles. Nobody was thrilled about it, least of all our techs, but those cameras ended up protecting them and us from bogus lawsuits. As we grew, people started targeting our trucks, hoping to cash in with false claims. That's what happens when you're successful, especially in service. Those "annoying" and expensive cameras saved us from at least three or four accidents that could have been wrongly blamed on us, along with $30,000 to $40,000 in legal fees *each time*. What felt like a headache at first turned out to be one of our smartest moves.

My point is these detours didn't just keep us moving; they often made us better, even if we didn't see it at the time. That's the mindset you need as an entrepreneur. Every roadblock is just a detour in disguise, and every detour is a hidden opportunity to improve—sometimes in ways you'd never see coming.

It wasn't just Green Mango that hit roadblocks and took detours.

Take Coconut Cleaning, our residential cleaning company. When COVID-19 hit in March 2020, Evan, who ran the operation, was convinced the company was done for.

"We're nonessential," he told me, his voice tight with panic as he paced the conference room. "We legally can't operate."

At the time, businesses deemed "nonessential" faced fines, closure, even public shaming if they simply tried to continue operating. The working world had transformed overnight. Gyms blacked out their windows and snuck in select clients through back doors. Thousands of restaurants did the same or closed permanently. Even parks, beaches, and playgrounds sat empty behind caution tape and barricades.

According to a March 2020 survey by the National Federation of Independent Business, nearly 92 percent of small businesses reported being negatively impacted. Worse, studies estimate that 200,000 to 400,000 US small businesses closed *permanently* due to the pandemic. That's up to 66 percent higher than the norm.

For our residential cleaning company, COVID felt like a death sentence. Who wanted strangers in their homes during a global pandemic? The very idea of letting someone pull into your driveway, let alone step inside, had become unthinkable. Customers were calling to make sure we *wouldn't* show up.

We paused all operations. The phones eventually fell silent. Revenue evaporated as days turned to weeks. I had to break the hard truth to Evan. "We have two months of runway, tops," I warned. "Then we're done." Two months until we'd have to fire everyone, including ourselves.

As cash reserves dwindled toward zero, most would have surrendered. Evan, however, wouldn't quit. Instead, he asked the question that changed everything: "What could make a cleaning company essential during a global pandemic?"

He pored over CDC guidelines, public health orders, and exemption clauses, searching for a lifeline like a needle in a haystack. Then, finally, he found it. Janitorial services were essential; more specifically, those that reduced viruses.

He dug deeper and uncovered something he'd never heard of before: *virucides*, or specialized cleaning agents designed to kill viruses on contact. The next morning, Evan showed up at our supplier's warehouse with a printout of the exact virucide they supposedly carried, the one that could theoretically deem us "essential" and put us back in business.

The warehouse manager barely looked up. "Yeah, it's back there on that shelf," he said, nodding toward a dusty corner lined with rows of untouched bottles. This supplier primarily specialized in restoration equipment and carpet-cleaning machines. Little did they know, those forgotten bottles were our lifeline.

"How much do you have?" Evan asked.

The employee tapped at the keyboard, squinted at the screen, and paused. "Looks like we've got 105 gallons left nationwide."

Evan's eyes widened. "I'll take it all."

Not only was Coconut back in business, but one week

later, the virucide distributor called Evan directly to let him know that the product he'd bought was the first EPA-approved solution proven to kill the COVID-19 strain of coronavirus. Guess who owned the entire supply?

What started as a desperate detour became rocket fuel. In just 10 months, Coconut Cleaning's fleet exploded from five vans to 15 to keep up with demand. Revenue soared from $1.7 million to $5 million. We nearly tripled our revenue during the worst economic crisis in decades.

This wasn't some pandemic fluke. Coconut was already on the rise before COVID, and the momentum only grew. The very next year, we hit a record $6.1 million in revenue.

That's the power of a detour. Where others saw a dead end —"we're nonessential"—Evan uncovered a hidden path forward.

The thing is, he wasn't even trying to strike gold. He was simply refusing to accept defeat. He, like me, wouldn't quit.

## Roadblocks Are Inevitable No Matter Who You Are or How Big You Get

In 2018, Tesla was in crisis mode. Elon Musk had promised investors 5,000 Model 3 sedans per week, but the company was dangerously behind schedule.

Wall Street analysts started circling like vultures. Short sellers bet millions that Tesla would flame out. The company was burning through $6,500 per minute. The stock had plunged nearly 40 percent in mere months as industry veterans began writing the automaker's obituary. Even Musk later admitted he feared the company would die.

Facing what he called "production hell," Musk made a move that flew in the face of every auto manufacturing playbook since Henry Ford. He told his team to build an entirely new assembly line...under a *tent* in the parking lot.

The 150,000-square-foot structure, larger than two football fields, was thrown together in mere weeks using scrap equipment and spare parts pulled from warehouses.

In an industry where new production lines typically take years and hundreds of millions of dollars to build, experts called it insanity. One analyst said, "Words fail me." Another joked they'd need a second tent just to fix the mistakes from the first.

Musk, on the other hand, tweeted this: "Not sure we actually need a building. This tent is pretty sweet." By August 2018, Tesla hit its goal: 5,000 Model 3s per week—thanks to that "pretty sweet" tent.

## Ask Yourself the Million-Dollar Question

What do Green Mango, Coconut Cleaning, Tesla, Apple, and almost every other success story have in common?

Detours.

One day, Steve Jobs stormed into the cubicle of Larry Kenyon, the engineer working on the Macintosh operating system. Jobs wasn't happy. The Mac was taking too long to boot up.

Kenyon started to explain why reducing the boot time wasn't possible, but Jobs cut him off.

"If it would save a person's life, could you find a way to shave 10 seconds off the boot time?"

Kenyon paused...and admitted he probably could.

Jobs grabbed a whiteboard and ran the numbers. If five million Mac users were wasting 10 extra seconds a day, that added up to over five million hours per year. That's the equivalent of more than seven lifetimes, or seven lives lost every year, he declared.

A few weeks later, Kenyon delivered by shaving a whopping 28 seconds off the boot time. That was nearly triple what Jobs had asked for and nearly triple what Kenyon himself had suggested was next to impossible.

That's the mindset you need.

When you hit a roadblock, don't just look for a way around it. Assume there is one, and go find it.

Whenever I was stuck, I'd ask myself: *If someone offered me $1 million to solve this problem by tomorrow, how would I do it?*

It didn't matter how big or small the problem was; the question remained the same. If you want to build a business that sells and blow past the roadblocks, you need to treat every detour like your future depends on it, because it does.

When you take it to the extreme—when you ask the million-dollar question about a thousand-dollar problem—suddenly, excuses disappear, obstacles shrink, creativity flips on, and detours appear out of thin air.

That mindset is how we found trucks when no bank would lend to us. It's how we kept our routes running when those trucks were suddenly uninsured. It's how Evan saved a multimillion-dollar company. It's how Tesla turned a tent into a production miracle. And it's how I turned $4.4 million in debt into more than $100 million in exits.

The million-dollar question forces you to find a way.

So ask yourself: *If I had $1 million on the line...if someone's life depended on it...or if seven lives depended on it...wouldn't I find a detour?*

When roadblocks pop up, don't stop. Find another way. You might end up at a destination even better than the one you had in mind.

Like Jobs said, "I'm convinced that about half of what separates the successful entrepreneurs from the non-successful ones is pure perseverance."

The million-dollar question is your lifeline. It's the secret weapon that keeps you moving, persevering, when everyone else quits.

But what happens when a $4.4 million problem makes a million-dollar one look like a rounding error?

Then what?

If John hadn't bailed on us, believe it or not, Green Mango would have never become what it did.

Those two years running five companies—and eventually a sixth—weren't wasted. Far from it. I accumulated more experience from 2016 to 2018 than most entrepreneurs do in a lifetime. If you count On the Spot, I'd lived seven business lives guiding seven different companies before my 30th birthday.

I had so much I could give Green Mango, but I had to stop taking from it first.

Trying to keep six businesses afloat was like trying to fuel six cars with one tank of gas. We couldn't get anywhere. I was scattered, Dusty was scattered, the team was scattered, even my life was scattered.

Clearly, we couldn't keep moving.

And that's the whole purpose of detours: They keep you moving.

John backing out forced me to stop chasing so many ventures at once. It compelled me to focus—really focus—on the one business that mattered most, the one I had the most stake in: Green Mango.

Remember, what you focus on expands. When I focused on Green Mango, it became far more valuable than all five of the other businesses combined.

The worst thing turned out to be the best thing. The roadblock became the detour.

The way I see it, the $4.4 million forced my hand. It obliged me to sell or shut down the distractions. If I hadn't, *they* would have shut down Green Mango. After all, it was floating *their* payroll and paying *their* debts.

It forced me to refocus on Green Mango—and that pushed me to empower others, like Evan, to operate Coconut Cleaning.

In turn, Green Mango and Coconut Cleaning *both* thrived.

The crazy thing is, I can trace it back even further. The recession that grounded my father's helicopter and my big dreams wasn't a roadblock after all. It was the first in a series of detours that led me exactly where I needed to go.

Pest control wasn't my dream, but it turned out to be the ultimate detour.

Nothing went according to plan, yet everything turned out better than I could have ever imagined. All because I kept finding detours, and therefore, I kept moving.

At the end of the day, your business is only as strong as the mindset of the person steering it. The systems, the people, the marketing—none of it matters without the driver in the seat.

A Lamborghini without a driver is just a parked car. A helicopter without a pilot is just dead weight on the tarmac.

Your mindset is everything. It decides whether you sit idle or soar. Whether you stall or go full throttle. Whether you stop at the roadblocks or uncover the detours that keep you moving.

The road ahead will have roadblocks—count on it. But the detours appear for those who refuse to stop. So keep going, keep moving; every step you take leaves another quitter behind. When you just keep moving, nothing can stop you. So what if you never stopped? What if, instead of quitting, you always found another way?

I can tell you from 14 years of experience that you'd win. No matter what. That's exactly what I did.

*Keep going.*

## Chapter Summary

- A winner is just a loser who tried one more time.
- Winners don't stop at roadblocks. They find detours and keep going.
- When stuck, ask the million-dollar question: *If someone offered me $1 million to solve this by tomorrow, how would I do it?*
- Perseverance—not intelligence—is what separates successful entrepreneurs from the rest.
- The only thing that guarantees failure is quitting.

THREE

SYSTEMS


*"At its core, a fully functioning business is basically a set of
systems and processes."*
–John Jantsch


I couldn't stop watching them. It was our third time at Great Wolf Lodge, and while my kids were lost in the magic of water slides, wave pools, and Dippin' Dots, I found myself laser-focused on something else: the lifeguards.

Something about them seemed...off.

Every single one of them—across the entire indoor water park—was constantly moving. Not just scanning the pool but pacing, twisting, backpedaling, dipping their heads in a rhythmic, almost robotic motion.

They were never still, never zoned out, never distracted. And I'd never seen anything like it.

You know what lifeguards usually look like: bored teenagers, slouched in their chairs, half-watching the water, half-scrolling Instagram.

Not at Great Wolf Lodge.

For three visits, I'd been captivated by their curious behavior. The first time, I chalked it up to teens being teens. By the second, it was too consistent to ignore. I recorded videos on my phone just to confirm I wasn't imagining it. This time, I had to know why.

I approached one of the lifeguards—a girl, maybe 19, dressed in full "wolfpack" gear. A red rescue tube was tucked under her arm, a hip pack was strapped around her waist, and a bright red whistle rested between her lips as she moved in perfect unison with her counterpart at the other end of the pool.

"Hey," I said, "why do you guys keep moving like that?"

She didn't make eye contact with me. She didn't even break rhythm. Her lips barely parted from her whistle as she offered a simple but profound reply: *"We're just trained that way."*

Then just like that, she was gone, pacing away. There was no time for chit-chat; she was locked in.

That's when it hit me: I was watching a *system* at work.

This wasn't about Great Wolf Lodge getting lucky with who they hired or stumbling into a group of well-raised teens who genuinely cared.

This was training. This was protocol. This was a system. And the system worked.

In the United States, drowning is the leading cause of death for children one to four years old (surpassing common tragedies like car accidents, choking, and poisoning). Globally, one person drowns roughly every two minutes, and one child drowns every four to five minutes.

Not at Great Wolf Lodge.

Despite dozens of locations welcoming millions of guests each year, not one person has drowned in nearly a generation.

At Great Wolf Lodge, high school kids, many working their very first jobs, operate like seasoned pros. Their system is the difference between life and death. Watching it in action, I had to ask myself: If a bunch of teenagers could master a system, why couldn't I?

Because they had one. And I didn't.

For years, I was running Green Mango like a water park without systems. Waves of problems would roll in, crash down, and drag me under. Every day, I was putting out fires, racing from crisis to crisis, hoping my team would figure it out.

Hope isn't a system. Neither is hearsay.

At first, I told myself, "This is just business." But that was a lie. If you're stuck in the same cycle, you're lying to yourself too. As serial entrepreneur Dan Martell says, "No one sets out to become an overstressed workaholic with declining health and relationships."

Did *you?*

One morning, I looked in the mirror and barely recognized myself. My face was puffier, my eyes looked tired, my shirts were choking my body. I had ballooned from a lean 190 to a bloated 220. I looked like crap and felt terrible.

Worse, I was frustrated with my employees. Frustrated with repeating myself. Frustrated with...*everything.*

More than half a decade in, I was *still* grinding 15 to 18 hours a day just to keep the wheels from falling off. Instead of running my business, I was frantically sprinting from one fire to the next.

And for what? Was this what success was supposed to feel like?

"Entrepreneurs end up there," Martell explains, "because they lack tested systems that deal with the unique challenges founders face." He was right. I lacked systems, and I was paying the price.

MY NUMMI MOMENT

We entrepreneurs have been learning this lesson the hard way for decades. I was no exception.

Neither was General Motors.

In 1984, GM's Fremont Assembly Plant was the worst auto plant in America. Not one of the worst. *The* worst. Cars rolled off the line missing steering wheels, workers drank on the job, some gambled in the breakroom, others skipped their shifts altogether. More than a few crawled into the cars on the line to sleep it off, then sabotaged vehicles just for fun. The place operated more like a dive bar trying to build cars than a real production plant.

General Motors had no choice but to shut the whole thing down. Then Toyota stepped in.

Surprisingly, Toyota didn't burn the plant to the ground, it didn't clean house, and it didn't even replace management. Toyota changed one thing: the systems.

Same people. Same plant. Same tools. Completely different result.

Within a year, the Fremont Assembly Plant went from

dead last to one of the best-performing in the United States. It was renamed NUMMI—New United Motor Manufacturing, Inc.—and it became a case study in what happens when you stop blaming people and start installing systems.

If systems could turn the worst factory in America into one of the best, what could they do for my business? My health? My family? My life? More importantly, what could systems do for yours?

At Green Mango, I desperately needed my own NUMMI moment.

# THE BIG THREE: WHAT EVERY GREAT SYSTEM IS BUILT ON

In the early days, Dusty and I wore every hat in the business. If something broke, we fixed it. If someone called, we answered. If a tech didn't show up, we jumped on the route.

I used to think running a business meant putting out fires, until I realized I was the one handing out matches.

Since our first hires were mostly technicians, they brought our first headaches. They missed call-aheads, showed up without the right products, and left without spraying the full perimeter of the home. Some even forgot to lock the customers' gates on their way out.

Our first instinct was to blame them.

We thought we'd hired the wrong guys since these were seemingly simple, obvious mistakes. Turns out, we were the ones who were dead wrong. Those mistakes were only simple and obvious *to us*. That was the problem. We knew how to do everything, but it was all trapped inside the one place no one else could access: our brains.

After each mistake, we talked through it with each tech

again and again. I felt like a broken record, hoping it would finally stick. But it never did, and it was the most frustrating thing ever. My blood pressure spiked every time my phone rang. It felt like *Groundhog Day* with bug spray. Same tech. Same issue. Same apology. "Don't forget to call ahead." "Don't forget the gate." I probably said those words more than I said "I love you" to Lyss for an entire year.

But conversations aren't systems.

I rotated between banging my head against the wall at my mom's house and pulling my own hair out. Meanwhile, the mistakes kept piling up, customers got mad, and we paid for it.

Ultimately, we had to fire people to put out the fires. That, ironically, meant throwing ourselves right back into the flames. Dusty and I were back on routes, spraying homes, and fighting every fire ourselves. The business couldn't grow because we were working *in* it, not *on* it. Like Maricopa all over again, we were trapped.

Inspired by the systems I saw when touring other service companies along with advice from established experts like Tommy Mello, I started writing everything down. Step by step. Start to finish. It sounds logical now, but it took me a long time to figure out.

Then one day, an ordinary sheet of paper became the foundation of our very first system: the Technician Route Execution Checklist.

The first version was basically scribbled on a napkin, but I kid you not, that simple checklist, that simple process of putting what was in my head down on paper, changed *everything*. Our techs now had a clear, foolproof list of what to do before, during, and after every route. From stocking the truck to logging chemicals to knocking on doors and closing customers' gates on their way out.

It made me realize Dusty and I had basically been barking plays without a playbook all along.

The day we handed that checklist to someone else, those familiar fires went out.

I got off the truck. So did Dusty. We could finally breathe and focus on growing the business instead of maintaining it. One checklist turned into three, three checklists turned into 10 pages. Ten pages turned into an entire Technician Manual built to, once and for all, prevent the problems we kept having to resolve. The best part is, that manual gave us time to focus on other areas of the business.

Premium service requires premium support, so our next priority was hiring customer service reps (CSRs) to handle scheduling and support calls. Dusty and I happily took off our CSR hats and handed new hires our next checklist.

It seemed like we'd figured it out.

But as we kept growing, new techs started making old mistakes.

A simple, preventable error—like forgetting to stock a product—could cause a tech to show up 10, 15, even 20 minutes late to their first appointment. That delay set off a chain reaction. The next three customers would call asking where their tech was. Those calls tied up our CSRs, which meant new customers couldn't get through to them. Frustrated, some canceled service altogether. Point is, one small mistake could cost hundreds a day and thousands a year. Worst of all, Dusty and I would end up right back in our trucks, spraying routes all over again.

Our systems were breaking down.

You see, by that point, our simple checklist had ballooned into a 29-page manual. And that massive manual was just one of three. Across all departments, we were pushing hundreds of pages of documentation. With so much documentation and so little training, we were basically expecting techs to read IKEA instructions one time and then build a bunk bed from memory.

As Confucius famously said, "What I hear, I forget. What I see, I remember. What I do, I understand."

Conversations were forgettable. Manuals were helpful, but training on what was inside the manuals became critical. We needed to practice the plays, not just diagram them. There was too much to know. Too much to do. We needed to *involve* people in the process.

Every great system, we learned, is built on three things: 1) Clear documentation 2) Repeatable training 3) Consistent auditing. Or, put simply, the Big Three: manuals, trainings, and audits.

If it's not written, trained, and checked, it's not a system.

Let's start at the top: getting it out of our heads and onto paper. For us, it all started with that checklist. Writing creates clarity and it flushes out the fluff. Like a small hinge swinging a big door, a single sheet of paper can change everything.

Without documentation, there's nothing to train. Without training, few can execute. Without audits, standards slip.

As we systematized every part of the business, we kept coming back to the Big Three. Every process was documented. Every role was trained. Every standard was audited. That's when the familiar fires disappeared for good and our systems held firm as we continued to grow.

Just to be clear, when I say documentation, I don't mean a dusty binder full of policies no one reads. I mean a living roadmap: one that shows every employee where they are, where we want them to be, and when they need to be there.

I equate it to training for an IRONMAN. You wouldn't just wing it. You'd hire a coach. That coach would give you a plan—what to do every day, how to track your pace and progress, and which milestones to hit along the way to make sure you're ready for race day. That's the power of the Big Three: Documentation lays out the path, training builds the skill, and auditing ensures everybody stays on track.

Before systems, we generated $1 to $2 million annual revenue with razor-thin margins and constant chaos. After systems, we generated $27 million in revenue, had 30 percent profit margins, and I even enjoyed a full month away in Thailand. (More on that in Chapter 8.)

For instance, we built a collections system that took our accounts receivable from 82 percent to a near-perfect 99 percent. That's a 17 percent lift on what eventually became $27 million in revenue, or an extra $4.6 million in cash flow. We shortened our service rotation from 10 weeks to eight weeks, and then to seven. Seeing customers more often meant billing more often, asking for referrals more often, upselling more often, skyrocketing service, and dramatically improving retention.

That one shift alone unlocked incredible growth. And to think, it all started with a simple checklist that cost me 30 minutes and a piece of notebook paper.

Without systems, you're stuck. Stuck in the truck. Stuck on the phone. Stuck fighting the same fires over and over. For us, it meant stuck at that $1 to $3 million plateau where about 97 percent of businesses get trapped.

Sure, you can grind your way to your first million or two, like we did, through sweat equity and free advertising. But eventually, you run out of time. You burn out fighting the same fires.

Then what?

You hire people, but without systems, people don't solve problems...they *create* them.

Just ask General Motors.

As Michael Gerber said, "Systems permit *ordinary* people to achieve *extraordinary* results predictably."

The more you systematize, the less you'll have to put out fires. The more you document, train, and audit, the more freedom you'll unlock. Systems are the smallest hinges that swing the biggest doors. Sometimes all it takes is a checklist on a napkin to get you started and get unstuck.

# SYSTEMS ARE FREEDOM

I'm no Jeff Bezos, but let's be real: Amazon isn't worth $2 trillion because Bezos himself is sprinting between fulfillment centers, loading Prime trucks, or boxing up your latest impulse buy. Just like I wasn't spraying homes anymore as we installed more and more systems, Toyota's CEO isn't manning the assembly line. Great Wolf Lodge's 80-something-year-old founder, Jack, isn't pacing the pool deck with the lifeguards.

Amazon's systems scaled the company from an online bookstore to the most dominant retailer on earth. Toyota's systems transformed the worst auto plant in America into one of the best. Great Wolf Lodge's systems made drowning virtually impossible at its water parks across North America. And our systems took me from spraying homes in Maricopa to making core memories on another continent.

Systems are your key to freedom.

If that's not enough reason to start building them yesterday, here's even better news: They also drive the highest business valuations.

# IS YOUR BUSINESS TURNKEY OR KEY-MAN?

Most entrepreneurs know what their business is worth to them. What they don't know is what it's worth to a buyer. That's where systems separate the winners from everyone else.

The term *key-man* started in business insurance to describe the financial risk of losing a critical individual. Today, it's shorthand for a dealbreaker and a line item buyers scrutinize.

Think of it like buying a house with just one support beam. If that beam cracks, the whole thing collapses. That's key-man risk in a business.

Buyers don't want to inherit your constant stress, your sleepless nights, or your firefighter-in-chief role. And they certainly don't want to pay for it. Would you?

That's why buyers want *systems*.

This means you and the buyer want the same thing. You want freedom. They want stability. They want a business that doesn't need you. You want a business someone will pay a premium to own. Systems give you both.

Systems are the ultimate two-for-one deal. They free you today and make you richer tomorrow. Think of systematizing your business like renovating your home: You get to enjoy the upgrades now, *and* they drive up the price when you sell.

I've heard others suggest systematized businesses sell for two to three times more than owner-reliant ones. That's the difference between a $10 million payday and a $30 million one. Between walking away with life-changing money or leaving tens of millions on the table. One gets you the Lambo, the other gets you the private jet *and* the Lambo. One gets you courtside seats, the other gets you a piece of the team. One sets *you* up for life, the other sets *your kids* up for theirs.

When buyers started analyzing Green Mango, they didn't see key-man risk. They saw the exact opposite: a turnkey operation. A machine that ran itself. That's why when offers started coming, they poured in, one after another. That's why our buyer, PestCo, made me an offer I couldn't refuse.

So if you're still doing everything yourself, ask yourself this: Are you building a business you have to run forever, or are you building something worth buying?

Systems save lives. They save companies. They save time. They solve problems. And when the time comes, they unlock buyers' checkbooks—generating offers you truly can't refuse.

You don't have to be Amazon, Toyota, or Great Wolf Lodge to reap the rewards. From landscaping to SaaS, HVAC to e-commerce and everything in between, systems are the key to sanity, scaling, selling, and freedom.

# SYSTEMATIZE YOUR BUSINESS IN 5 SIMPLE STEPS

*Ready. Fire. Aim.* Let's start building your systems right now. Whether you want to scale, sell, or simply reclaim your time, these five steps will help you build systems that run without you.

## Step 1: Start Small and Keep It Simple

Big systems are built one page at a time. You don't need a 100-page manual tomorrow. Instead, you just need one page that solves one real problem. Start with the one task that's slowing you down or stealing your sleep right now, i.e., the fire that keeps reappearing. Write down how you'd solve it, break it into steps, make each step clear, and remember, done is better than perfect.

The key is to keep it simple. Picture any car. The gas is on the right; the brake is on the left. Your systems should be just as simple and just as natural.

As my guy Tommy Mello says, "You have to get those procedures out of your head and in writing, so people don't have to read your mind." If it's not written, it's not real. And if you can't write it down, it's already too complex.

At Green Mango, we stored every system in the employee training platform Trainual for instant digital access. Plus, we always had hard copies on hand too. Your employees should never have to hunt your systems down. Easy access drives adoption.

## Step 2: Train Like You Fight

The US military says, "Train like you fight, fight like you train." Navy SEALs typically train for 18 months before their first deployment. The Marine Corps emphasizes training at full speed, not half-speed. My friend Jamie, a former SWAT operator, trained daily for 15 years. Now, even in private security, he still trains daily.

At Green Mango, we trained every single week. For example, technicians trained on service execution, managers trained on leadership, and CSRs trained on our service systems. Without training, a system is just a bunch of words on a page.

Even a potential buyer once told me, "Become a training company." That's what we did.

## Step 3: Retrain Through Rotations

Amazon follows Bezos' philosophy that "Every day is Day One." That means employees aren't trained once and sent on their way. They're constantly retrained to stay sharp. At Green Mango, we did the same thing through what we called training rotations.

Here's how our rotations worked: Every department held a weekly training. Each week's topic changed based on a preset, rotating schedule tailored to that department's needs.

For example, our sales department ran a six-week rotation to cover the full sales process:

- **Week 1**: Buyer psychology and problem discovery
- **Week 2**: Building rapport
- **Week 3**: Framing and pitching your offer
- **Week 4**: Closing techniques
- **Week 5**: Upsells and referrals
- **Week 6**: Follow-up

After Week 6, we'd cycle back to Week 1 and begin again, ensuring constant reinforcement and refinement.

I'm not saying all your training rotations have to be six weeks. The key is to identify your critical systems and build a rotating schedule that covers them all in a logical, repeatable sequence. If you have 18 systems to cover, and you want a six-week rotation, train on three systems or topics per week. As you develop new systems, slot corresponding trainings into your rotation.

That's how you keep everyone sharp, and it's how you turn training into a system of its own.

## Step 4: Audit Often

People do what you *inspect*, not what you *expect*.

Systems fail when no one checks if they're being followed. That's why we ran regular audits across every department. Now, you don't need to run out and hire a full-time auditor tomorrow. Instead, start by having your managers audit other departments today. For instance, you could have sales leaders audit techs, ops managers audit CSRs, and vice versa.

We didn't audit our systems early on because I didn't know any better. That's why, even with documented systems and regular training, we kept running into the same problems I thought we'd already solved. I eventually discovered, almost every time, the root issue was the same: People had stopped following the system designed to prevent it.

It's no different than students acting up the second the teacher leaves the room. Without accountability, even great employees do their own thing, rarely realizing the ripple effect it can cause.

But once we put regular audits in place, everything changed. I'd walk into a department six months later and find things still running exactly how I designed them. That had never happened before, and I can't even begin to explain how satisfying it was. Best of all, the business benefitted. When I eventually sold Green Mango, our EBITDA margin had climbed from the low 20s to north of 29 percent, and I credit a big chunk of that to auditing our systems.

As soon as you have an employee expected to follow a system, have someone consistently checking. I wish we'd started auditing from day one. It would've saved me all kinds of stress and helped us hit higher margins even faster.

## Step 5: Measure Results

Auditing without measuring is like showing up to the gym without tracking your weights. You're doing the reps, but are you actually getting stronger?

If audits confirm systems are being followed, measuring the results proves those systems are making a difference. Together, auditing and measuring form a feedback loop that transforms good systems into great ones while exposing the ones that need to be rebuilt.

Take our Technician Route Execution Checklist. Audits ensured techs followed the process before and during each route, but measuring meant zooming out and asking: Did reservice rates decrease? Did customer complaints go down? Did referrals or upsells increase?

Same thing with sales training. Week 4 of our rotation focused on closing. Audits made sure everyone was present and engaged, but measuring our close rate was what proved that the training was paying off.

Think: Is the system saving time? Reducing errors? Increasing revenue? Pick one to two simple metrics per system and track them consistently.

# SYSTEMATIZE EVERYTHING

Eventually, at Green Mango, systems ran everything—and I mean *everything*.

Take referrals, for example. We didn't just tell our team to ask for referrals. We handed them a script with specific talking points. Dress code? Covered. The hose color? Always black. The holster? Always green. Even our marketing packets were systematized right down to the order of each insert. How many times to call, text, and email a customer; when to follow up; what to say and do at every step—it was all systematized, audited, and measured.

Learn from my mistakes by starting today.

Systems run the business, but people run the systems.

That's why, next, I'll show you how we built a world-class team that looked forward to coming to work every day, treated customers and colleagues like family, and eventually scaled our systems into a $27 million machine.

## Chapter Summary

- Systems are freedom.
- Buyers pay premiums for turnkey businesses, not key-man risks.
- Every great system is built on "The Big Three": 1) Clear documentation 2) Repeatable training 3) Consistent auditing.
- If it's not written, trained, and checked, it's not a system.
- Systematize everything: Start small. Train like you fight. Retrain through rotations. Audit often. Measure results.

FOUR

PEOPLE


*"Your people are your product."*
–Richard Branson


"I'd like to offer you a job."

She blinked. "I already have one."

I was standing in line at Dutch Bros Coffee, watching the most engaged, enthusiastic employee I'd ever seen smiling and laughing, calling customers by name, and effortlessly whipping up drinks without missing a beat.

She had *it*. The thing every business owner dreams of.

At the time, I was in recruiting mode 24/7. We were burning through techs and CSRs like crazy. We'd hire one and lose two. The churn was killing us. Everywhere I went, I kept my eyes peeled for talent.

And there she was: the kind of employee we desperately needed. The kind of employee I knew I could get. Surely, she wasn't making much more than minimum wage at Dutch Bros. So I made her an offer—more money than they would ever pay her.

She, to my surprise, didn't even hesitate. "No thanks," she said politely, smiling. "I'm happy here."

I was stunned. Who turns down more money just like that?

I had to know why. "I make minimum wage," she explained. "But I love the people here. I love the *culture*."

I'll never forget that moment. I had spent years throwing money at employee churn, convinced pay was the solution. Culture, I found out that day, is worth more than money.

It got me thinking, *What would our company look like if every employee felt that way?*

What would yours look like?

I thought I needed to outspend everyone else to attract and retain top talent, but that barista opened my eyes to the truth: I needed to focus on culture instead.

Culture doesn't just keep incredible employees happy at minimum wage gigs. Culture builds careers. It builds companies. It can even reshape billion-dollar empires overnight.

Just ask Disney.

In 2006, Disney acquired Pixar for $7.4 billion. At the time, the deal raised eyebrows. Pixar had produced just seven films in its entire history. Disney, on the other hand, was already releasing more films in a single year than Pixar had in its lifetime.

So why spend billions?

It wasn't just the technology. It wasn't even the characters. According to Disney CEO Bob Iger, the real asset was Pixar's culture. Rather than folding Pixar into Disney, Iger wanted Pixar's culture to breathe new life into Disney itself.

In fact, he appointed Pixar's cofounder Ed Catmull and creative head John Lasseter to lead Walt Disney Animation Studios, ensuring Pixar's culture guided Disney's creative future.

Think about that.

Leading up to the acquisition, Pixar CEO Steve Jobs famously warned Iger of perhaps his biggest fear, writing, "Disney's culture will destroy Pixar!" across a whiteboard.

Catmull said the same thing differently, stressing that culture beats strategy repeatedly. Lasseter added, "Pixar is not about computers, it's about people."

Disney's investment in Pixar and its people-first culture paid off handsomely.

By 2010, just four short years after the acquisition, Pixar led an animation revival for Disney, generating more than $4 billion at the box office following a string of hits including *Cars, Ratatouille, WALL-E,* and *Up.*

In 2021, Green Mango was Disney and Coconut Cleaning was Pixar.

That year, we made what seemed like a minor logistical decision: We'd split the annual holiday party event by company.

Coconut would have its party first, and Green Mango would follow. I expected two different parties. After all, Coconut had just 32 employees at the time. Even with plus-ones, we'd have maybe 64 people in the room. Green Mango, on the other hand, would easily pack the same space with nearly 300 people.

Still, I didn't expect the same room to feel like two completely different worlds. And I definitely didn't expect Coconut's party to feel how Green Mango's *should.*

If you've ever been to a professional golf tournament, you know most are hushed, proper affairs with quiet whispers and polite, restrained applause. Think "golf claps." If you've ever been to the Waste Management Open in Scottsdale, you know it's the exact opposite.

Even if nobody breaks par, everybody's partying.

That was Coconut's holiday party.

It was electric. You could *feel* the energy in the room. Anytime Evan, my partner at Coconut, called an employee up to the front of the room to receive an award, the place erupted. Picture every single employee *and* their plus-ones leaping to their feet. Evan could barely finish a sentence on the mic. The people took over. They hugged. They took videos. They pounded tables. Inside jokes flew across the room like confetti. It was like witnessing a hole-in-one at the Waste Management Open. Every. Single. Time. The collective energy could've powered Phoenix for a week.

I lingered for a moment, soaking it in. It felt like winning. It felt alive.

If Coconut's party was the Waste Management Open, Green Mango's was Sunday at the Masters—the most buttoned-up day in professional golf. At Augusta National, where the Masters is held, they don't have fans; they have "patrons." Running is prohibited. Cheering too loudly will get you escorted out. In 2018, "Dilly Dilly!"—a harmless Bud Light catchphrase—was reportedly on a list of banned sayings that would get you removed immediately. In other words, the event is run by the fun police.

When I called Green Mango employees to the front of the very same room to receive their awards, all I heard was golf claps.

People clapped because they were supposed to and smiled because they were supposed to. They accepted their awards, nodded appreciatively, and sat back down right on cue. There were no inside jokes. No standing ovations. No banging on tables.

Driving home that night, I couldn't stop thinking about the contrast. I couldn't unsee it. I had built both Green Mango and Coconut Cleaning from the ground up, yet somewhere along the way, Green Mango had become a place where winning didn't even feel like it. At the time, Green Mango was a behemoth compared to Coconut. If anything, Coconut was its redheaded stepchild. Yet the stark difference between the two company cultures was clear as day, and it left me gutted.

What was missing? We had the talent, the resources, and the systems, but we were still losing where it mattered most—with the people.

Though culture may sound soft (as it once did to me), it carries a price tag in the billions.

In the US alone, toxic workplaces cost businesses nearly $1 trillion a year in lost productivity and turnover. Meanwhile, companies that prioritize culture experience a significant 33 percent increase in revenue.

Even in golf, the tournament with the loudest, most engaged, most raving fans is both the most fun…and the most valuable.

Believe it or not, the Waste Management Open generates nearly four times the economic impact of The Masters—a stunning $465 million in 2024 versus an expected $120 million for the Augusta event.

So why do we run our businesses like the Masters? Why was I running Green Mango this way?

Between that deflating conversation at Dutch Bros and the culture clash I witnessed at the back-to-back holiday parties, I knew something had to change. I had to change the culture. And I was determined to.

We spend more time at work than we do at home, and for too long, I had settled for a culture that just checked the box.

I decided to tackle culture the way I tackle everything: systematically.

At Green Mango, we were losing 176 technicians every year before implementing what I now call our Culture Cornerstones. Soon after, that number dropped to just 76. We cut turnover by more than half, saving hundreds of thousands in hiring and training costs. Beyond the numbers, what I valued most was walking into a building that finally felt alive. A workplace where people felt at home.

I could go on and on about culture and the many ways to drive it. Truth be told, I rushed out and bought a basketball hoop, massage chairs, and Xboxes for the office within days of being rejected at Dutch Bros. While those things can make a difference, they're not enough to drive world-class culture on their own. Let's go beyond the obvious and expected by focusing on the three Culture Cornerstones that made the biggest difference at Green Mango, because I believe they'll make the biggest difference in your business too.

THE THREE CULTURE
CORNERSTONES

Every business has a culture whether they design it or not. The difference between a business that thrives and one that struggles comes down to how intentionally that culture is built. Let's break down how we built a world-class culture at Green Mango.

## Culture Cornerstone #1: The Rule of 7

Five years into Green Mango, I hired a friend's younger brother as one of our first 10 technicians. He showed up early, never missed a shift, and never asked for anything. He was steady. Quiet. Solid. The definition of reliable. He kept to himself and did his thing, eventually growing alongside the company as we elevated him to the role of specialty technician.

At the time, I believed in maintaining professional boundaries with our team. Business was business. Personal was personal. We never discussed his hobbies, his family dynamics, or his aspirations beyond Green Mango. In my eyes, he was the epitome of a model technician and that was all I needed to know.

Then, one day, he didn't show up for work. I called once. Twice. Three times. Each unanswered ring felt heavier than the last.

Eventually, my phone buzzed. It was my buddy—his older brother.

"My brother"—he paused—"committed suicide." Right then, my entire world came to a screeching halt. What did we miss? What didn't we do? What could we have done? What could *I* have done?

It was the first time it truly hit me just how much influence we have as business owners. We help shape people's lives, for better or worse. Our culture, our environment, our leadership approach—it all matters more than I'd ever realized.

That call changed me. Forever. It changed how I ran my business forever, too. How could it not?

Sadly, we had a workplace where someone could show up every day, do everything right, and still feel completely alone without anyone knowing it.

While culture still felt abstract at the time, from then on I was determined to make sure no one in my company ever felt that alone again.

But I didn't know how until I heard one of the most respected military officers of our time break leadership down to a simple number: 7.

*"Human beings are generally not capable of managing more than six to 10 people, particularly when things go sideways."*
—Jocko Willink

In Ramadi, one of Iraq's most volatile war zones, Navy

SEALs found that leadership started failing when teams grew larger than seven.

Jocko Willink, the commander of Task Unit Bruiser, saw that when things went sideways, lives were lost.

So he restructured his entire unit into smaller teams, per what he called decentralized command. Our version of decentralized command was what I call the Rule of 7: No leader should have more than seven direct reports. After all, the sweet spot, Willink found, was four to six subordinates, who in turn must be able to effectively lead their own teams.

The impact was immediate, and the results were undeniable. Under this structure, Task Unit Bruiser became one of the most decorated special operations units of the Iraq War, earning numerous valor awards including Silver Stars, Bronze Stars, and Navy Commendation Medals. Seeing Task Unit Bruiser's success, other SEAL teams in Ramadi reportedly adopted the same decentralized command structure.

What works in war works in business and beyond.

Amazon has two-pizza teams: If a team is too big to be fed by two pizzas, it's too large. During Apollo 13, NASA's Mission Control relied on five-to-seven-person "tiger teams" to help save the crew. Intel used a similar philosophy to scale from $1.9 billion to $25 billion under Andy Grove. Grove suggested that a manager whose span of control exceeds eight subordinates will "suffer in effectiveness."

Essentially, leadership fails when it gets too big.

At Green Mango, no manager led more than seven people, period. It was a drastic shift that forced us to hire more managers and cost us hundreds of thousands per year in additional overhead. That said, what we gained was worth far more: retention, trust, and a true culture shift.

The biggest win, of course, is that we never lost a life again.

Suddenly, managers had time to truly know their people,

employees received faster responses to their needs, and no one felt like just another number. Most importantly, it gave everyone a sense of belonging—the feeling of having seven best friends at work rather than just another boss. As a result, company culture began to flourish.

Employees didn't just work for Green Mango anymore; they worked for their manager and their team. When they walked into work, they were greeted by seven friends eager to help and support them. They had camaraderie. Trust. Reciprocity. They operated with the precision of a SEAL team, and they had each other's backs, just like the baddest men on the planet do.

What wouldn't you do for your best friend?

Thanks to the Rule of 7, employees stopped quitting, they stopped calling out, and stopped giving anything less than their best. And that was just the beginning.

## IMPLEMENTING THE RULE OF 7

For every seven employees, there must be a manager. For every seven managers, there must be a leader above them. That's how you prevent failure at scale. It's not just about managing people; it's about knowing them. The moment an employee stops feeling seen is the moment they start looking for another job.

As you scale, you must be disciplined about splitting teams the right way. The second a manager had eight direct reports, we split the team—five and three, four and four—whatever made the most sense. The same went for management layers. Every employee always knew exactly who their leader was, and no more than seven people ever went to the same person for help. In this way, we found the Rule of 7 is the best thing for employees *and* managers.

Coconut Cleaning was proof. After implementing the Rule of 7, the business grew like crazy, and we did it without posting a single job opening for more than six years.

Every new hire came from referrals. Employees were so bought in that they invited friends and family to join. At one point, we had five sets of brothers working at Coconut. That's the true sign of a culture worth being part of.

## DO YOU REALLY KNOW YOUR PEOPLE?

Look at your org chart. How many direct reports do your managers have? If it's more than seven, I'd bet it all you have a culture problem.

Here's one way to stress-test it. Do your managers know their team members' spouses' names? How about their kids? Better yet, their dogs?

If not, they don't truly know their team. They're hitting the limits of human connection. And trust me, that's a risk no business can afford to take.

Remember, your people are more than employees.

## Culture Cornerstone #2: Recognition at Every Level

Workplace research shows employees who feel consistently recognized are *three times* more likely to be highly engaged and far less likely to quit than those who don't. In fact, a 10-year study of more than 200,000 employees found that frequent, meaningful recognition was the single greatest driver of workplace engagement—more than salary, benefits, or even job security. Simply put, recognition is the most underrated tool for performance and retention.

Yet most businesses get it all wrong.

Instead of making recognition a systematic part of how they operate, they either overcomplicate it (turning it into a stiff, HR-driven process) or they treat it as an obligation (picture those dusty, uninspiring employee-of-the-month plaques in break rooms across America).

As I learned, a single thank-you doesn't drive culture, a once-a-year award doesn't create loyalty, and a familiar pat on the back is basically worthless. Employees need to feel valued—consistently—in ways that matter to them.

To transform our good intentions into consistent action, we built what I now call the Recognition Matrix: a simple system that ensures recognition happens at three key levels, with each driving culture in its own way.

Let's break it down.


### RECOGNITION LEVEL 1: COMPANY-WIDE

At the company level, recognition needs to be consistent and scalable, but that doesn't mean it has to be generic. Sure, like most businesses, we celebrated birthdays and anniversaries at every company meeting. But let's face it, that's like the Xboxes and massage chairs—it's not enough.

Most companies hand out the same generic anniversary gift whether the employee wants it or not. We did the opposite by handing out Look Books. Each page had escalating rewards that employees could choose from on every work anniversary. Like a menu, they'd flip through the options and "order" the reward that excited them most.

Some went for AirPods, a new Keurig, or a Kindle. Others preferred a golf outing, a VR headset, or a KitchenAid mixer. Target shopping sprees and Amazon gift cards were always options, too.

As tenure grew, so did the choices. We offered electric

scooters, Dyson vacuums, MacBook Pros, Traeger grills, even ice barrels for cold plunges. The employees who stuck with us could eventually choose from a fully paid cruise, a Peloton bike, a new washer and dryer, or a trip to Vegas, San Diego, or even Disneyland.

The psychology was simple: What motivates one person doesn't motivate everyone. By giving choices, we showed we valued both their service and their individuality.

It's the difference between picking your own dream vacation and someone handing you plane tickets to a place you've never wanted to go.

If recognition is meant to be meaningful, why not let people choose what matters most to them?

## RECOGNITION LEVEL 2: DEPARTMENT-WIDE

At the department level, recognition should reinforce team goals and values while ideally creating visible symbols of achievement.

Partly inspired by the badges I'd earned in Scouts, we created badges technicians could earn and pin to their company-issued custom vests. Each badge was a bold, eye-catching symbol of achievement, a way to announce *"I earned this"* without saying a word.

The vest itself was just as cool as the badges. Jet-black. Tactical. Sleek. Each one had the technician's last name embroidered across the back.

The front of the vest became a visual resume of achievements. Every badge told a story from sales milestones and certifications to service anniversaries and more. The more badges you earned, the more respect you commanded.

Plus, each badge was designed to reinforce behaviors that moved the business forward. In this way, we were recognizing employees for achieving our business goals. That's the key—recognition and results should always align, so everybody wins.

For example, the Heat Check Badge was awarded to techs who powered through Arizona's brutal 115-degree summers without missing a single shift. They basically got to pin a flamethrower to their vests. Other badges focused more on mastery and longevity than attendance. Service 5,000 homes and they'd earn the 5K Homes Protected Badge, indicating they were among our most trusted, experienced pros. The Long Haul Badge went to the veterans—the guys who stayed loyal for five full years in an industry notorious for sky-high turnover.

Then there were badges that directly impacted the bottom line: dollar signs you could stack up as you closed more sales ($2K, $5K, $10K). Of course, we also recognized culture itself. Some guys weren't the top performers on paper, but they were the glue that held the team together. The Hype Man Badge went to them for making long days feel shorter, for keeping morale high, and for making work a place people actually *wanted* to be.

It didn't take long for competition to kick in. Nobody wanted an empty space where a badge should be. I'm a big believer in gamifying good habits. That vest, those badges, they made work a *game* people wanted to win.

Video games like Call of Duty have players grinding for hours just to earn a digital badge on the screen. We tapped into that same psychology, but for real work. By doing that, everybody won.

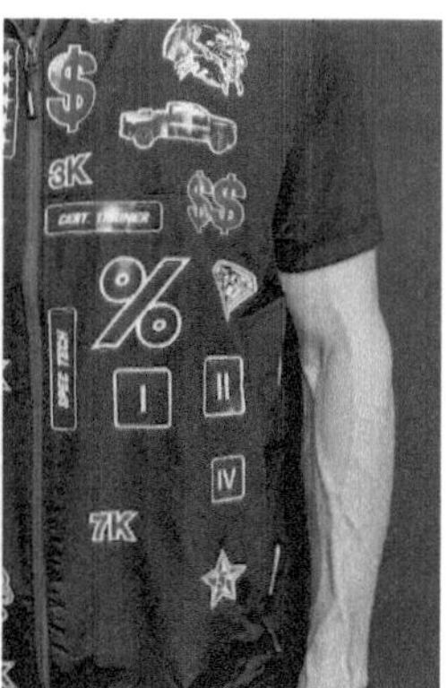

Green Mango technician vest

### RECOGNITION LEVEL 3: INDIVIDUAL

Finally, we implemented PPFs, or personal, professional, and financial goals, for every employee. Instead of guessing what would motivate someone, we asked them every quarter.

My friend Jason knows the power of this approach. One of his employees shared that her mother was losing her vision. She dreamed of taking her to Italy before it was too late. That employee worked hard, hit her targets, and instead of a generic bonus, Jason's company helped pay for their trip.

Another employee had spent years feeling self-conscious about his teeth. The procedure he wanted was always out of reach, so Jason bonused him a brand-new set of teeth. A clear sign of world-class culture, the employee's colleagues *chose* to chip in too. Some gave 10 bucks, others gave 100. Either way, the entire team came together to change one man's life.

You can't buy that kind of culture.

Before PPFs, I assumed everyone wanted what I wanted and liked what I liked: things like helicopter rides, trips to the dunes, and boating at Lake Powell.

I was dead wrong.

One employee wanted nothing more than Star Wars LEGO sets, so we made it happen. We gifted another guy a rock crawler to enjoy with his son on weekends. Nothing was off-limits because motivation isn't one-size-fits-all.

Taking a page from the book *The Carrot Principle* by Adrian Gostick and Chester Elton, we used PPFs to dangle custom carrots, tailoring recognition (carrots) to the individual.

Want to buy a house? Let's build a commission structure that helps you do it. Want to take your kid to Disneyland? Let's figure out a bonus system that makes it happen.

By rewarding employees with tailored recognition, on top of everything else, motivation skyrocketed, retention soared, and engagement exploded.

When you can connect what *they* want with what *you* need, everybody wins. PPFs make it easy to know exactly what each individual really wants.

Now here's where it all comes together.

## THE MATRIX EFFECT

When recognition happens at all three levels—company, department, and individual—and each level serves a specific purpose, the impact is infinite.

Let's take a technician named Mike. By his third year at Green Mango, Mike could experience all three levels of the Recognition Matrix.

He could choose a Traeger grill from the Look Book (company level), earn his Heat Check and 3K Homes Protected badges at our department meeting (team level), and through his PPF, we could discover his dream is to take his son hunting for the first time. When Mike exceeds his quarterly goals, we reward him with specialized hunting gear instead of a standard bonus (individual level).

Do you think Mike would up and leave Green Mango the next day?

Not a chance—Mike's a lifer.

Thanks to the Recognition Matrix, our employees felt valued by the organization (Level 1), respected by their peers (Level 2), and seen as individuals by their managers (Level 3).

## Culture Cornerstone #3: Right Bus, Right Seat

In *Good to Great*, author Jim Collins introduced the simple but profound idea of *right bus, right seat*. Your company is the bus, and the roles are the seats.

Picture a bus with everyone crammed up front or piled on just one side. The whole bus gets thrown off balance. The same goes for your company. Even with great people on board, if they're in the wrong seats, everything slows down—or worse, tips over.

However, when you get the right people into the right seats, you strike the perfect balance. The bus runs more smoothly, moves faster, and actually gets where you want it to go.

### WRONG BUS, RIGHT SEAT

Randy Moss was one of the most dominant wide receivers in NFL history, but in the 2006 season, you would have never known it. He was in the wrong place. The Oakland Raiders weren't a fit, the coaching wasn't a fit, the culture wasn't a fit. He caught just three touchdown passes all season. Fans dubbed him "washed up." He was approaching 30 years old, and even pundits predicted that his best years were behind him.

The very next season, Moss made history.

The New England Patriots picked him up and he exploded. In his first season with the team, Moss caught 23 touchdown passes, setting an all-time NFL record and helping lead the Patriots to an undefeated regular season.

Moss was in the right seat all along. Oakland was just the wrong bus.

It's easy to assume that when someone is underperforming, they're the problem. But sometimes it's not the player; it's the team.


## RIGHT BUS, WRONG SEAT

Julian Edelman was a college quarterback at Kent State, but when he entered the NFL, the Patriots moved him to wide receiver. A 5-foot-10 QB with zero experience filling a roster spot at receiver? Most teams wouldn't have bothered, but Edelman thrived. He became a key piece in three Patriots Super Bowl runs and even earned Super Bowl MVP honors in his new "seat."

He didn't need a different bus in the NFL. He just needed to move to a different seat.

At Green Mango, we saw this firsthand. Take James. He started as a technician and crushed it. Then he moved into management, where he was solid, but something was missing.

One day, he pulled me aside. "I need more growth," he said. "I feel stuck."

So I asked him to help out in the office.

At the time, we were struggling with route efficiency, and I knew James had an insider's perspective. He jumped into routing management and transformed the entire operation. He saw things the office team couldn't. He understood fall-off rates, completion issues, and scheduling inefficiencies in ways that completely changed how we ran the business.

Before, he was managing people. Now, he was managing the entire routing operation. He sat in a new seat and drove our bus to new heights. James was a key reason we achieved that seven-week service rotation that added $6 million per year to our bottom line, and it was all because he switched seats.

Ian, on the other hand, was one of our best technicians. He loved being in the field—problem-solving, working with his hands, helping customers.

When the opportunity opened, we promoted him to Field Manager. Six months later, he asked for something you'd never expect: *a pay cut.*

He hated management and missed the field. He desperately wanted to go back to killing bugs. We moved him back to his old seat and just like that, Ian was thriving again.

Both the bus *and* the seat matter.

Even great people can underperform when they're in the wrong role, but when you match talent to the right opportunity, everything clicks. That's when your team finds its rhythm, and people stop feeling like cogs in a machine and start feeling like difference-makers.

World-class culture requires the right people on the bus and every person in the right seat. And it's on you to make that happen.

# CULTURE IS A SYSTEM

When you combine all three Culture Cornerstones—the Rule of 7, the Recognition Matrix, and the Right Bus, Right Seat philosophy—something magical happens: People feel known, valued, and positioned to succeed.

That Dutch Bros barista showed me that my system was backwards. I'd been trying to solve people problems with money when I should have been investing money into culture.

Systems run the business, but people run the systems—and culture is the operating system that makes your people want to run them perfectly, every time.

What does world-class culture look like?

It looks like 150 people in charcoal and green, pounding tables, erupting in cheers, and high-fiving like every name called is their own. It looks like teammates chipping in to buy their co-worker new teeth. It looks like employees referring their own family to join the team. It looks like Star Wars LEGOs instead of helicopter rides. It looks like managers who know your dog's name.

It's a barista turning down a raise because she already has

what money can't buy. It's Randy Moss catching 23 touchdowns his first season in New England, and it's people staying on the bus and settling into the right seat.

That's how you build a culture where your best people turn down more money to stay. Where culture generates four times the economic impact while having four times more fun. Where every person has their perfect reward, their perfect role, their perfect team.

That's how you create something worth billions to someone who already has everything. That's how you build a business where systems and culture multiply each other's value.

That's how you build to sell.

# PRO TIPS FOR HIRING, LEADING, AND KEEPING THE BEST PEOPLE

From the very first moment someone hears about your company, every touchpoint afterward either strengthens or weakens your culture. The following pro tips helped us go from constant turnover to industry-leading retention and turn holiday parties into actual celebrations.

## Hire at the Right Time

Here's my rule of thumb, the 50 Percent Rule: If a new hire will cost you $4,000 per month, don't wait until you can afford the full $4,000. Hire them once you're consistently generating $2,000 per month (half their cost). Then use the time they free up to generate $4,000+ in new business.

Essentially, you're hiring people to take your seat so you can move into a more valuable one that covers their cost and then some.

## Where to Find the Best Hires

Not all recruiting sources are equal. I think of them like rungs on a ladder:

- **Bottom Rung**—Job sites (Indeed, Glassdoor): High volume, low signal. A numbers game.
- **Middle Rung**—Social media: Brand-driven. Show off your culture, energy, and edge.
- **Top Rung**—Referrals: Culture-driven. The clearest sign people love working for you.

Eventually, with a strong culture, referrals will do most of your recruiting for you. That's ideal because they're almost always your best hires.

## Sell *Them* on *You*

If you're still running interviews like it's 1995, you're losing top talent. Flip the model. Don't just vet candidates—sell *them* on *you*.

As Lou Adler often emphasizes, the best candidates have options; if you don't sell them on your company, someone else will.

Airbnb's former director of global recruiting, Jill Riopelle, knows this better than anyone. She recruited the organization's entire *internal* team to sell *external* candidates on working there. For example, Airbnb started recognizing the "Interviewer of the Week" at Friday meetings. In one instance, the hiring manager who went on a weekend hike to woo a top candidate was gifted a case of PBR beer in honor of the team's "ABR" (Always Be Recruiting) mantra. The company hand-wrote welcome notes to candidates on whiteboards in interview rooms. Even candidates who *weren't* hired were given a coupon if they advanced to a certain stage in the process as a thank-you from the company.

That's how serious this is.

The best people have options, so why should they choose you?

Treat your best candidates like your best customers: Sell them on your culture.

## Take Care of Your People, and They Will Take Care of You

When you invest in culture, you're investing in your company's most valuable asset: its people. The ROI on that is undeniable.

That's why this one simple line became my leadership mantra: "Take care of your people, and they will take care of you."

Systems run the business. People run the systems. Culture, though, is what makes them turn down twice the money to keep running yours.

## Chapter Summary

- Company culture is your most valuable asset.
- The best people won't leave for more money if they love where they work.
- Build culture intentionally with the Three Culture Cornerstones:
  - The Rule of 7—Small teams create deep connection.
  - The Recognition Matrix—Recognize employees at every level.

- o Right Bus, Right Seat—Match people to the roles they're built for.
- Culture is a system. Design it with the same care as your operations.
- Treat your best candidates like your best customers: Sell them on your culture.

FIVE

SALES

<br>

*"The purpose of business is to create and keep a customer."*
–Peter Drucker

H ave you ever knocked on a stranger's door and asked them to question everything they believe?

I have, more times than I can count.

For two years as a missionary, that was my job: selling the impossible to the uninterested. Picture a rail-thin teenager, just old enough to drive, trying to talk to grown adults about something as personal and taboo as faith on their doorstep. It was like trying to sell winter coats door-to-door in the middle of triple-digit Phoenix summers.

Worse, I wasn't confident or charismatic. I was nervous, shy, and monotone—the exact opposite of what the job called for. With every step toward the door, the pit in my stomach grew until it felt like the Grand Canyon had opened inside me.

Then, we launched Green Mango...and I was back on the doors.

Though more experienced, I was still nervous, still shy, and still monotone. Mio Energy Enhancers were my liquid courage. As I stood face-to-face with new doors, I'd dig that little plastic bottle out of my pocket and lick the spout to give myself a quick boost of caffeine and confidence. Forget the pit in my stomach; even with that jolt, it felt like a fishing lure was lodged in my throat by the time the door swung open.

If I didn't sell, we didn't eat. So despite my nerves, I kept knocking, practicing, and improving.

Over time, I built a system that transformed a terribly shy kid knocking on doors into a sales machine that grew to generate $27 million in annual revenue. A system so effective that one day, I didn't need to knock anymore. Eventually, we didn't need anyone knocking on a single door because prospects (and buyers) were knocking on *our* door instead.

At Green Mango, we didn't start with marketing because we didn't have the money to. Instead, we started with pure selling.

This chapter is about our journey from closing one customer to turning one into two and making two worth four. It's a simple three-step process I'll break down for you: Close. Duplicate. Multiply.

Let's get into Step 1: Close.

# STEP 1: CLOSE LIKE CLOCKWORK

My dad was right when he said, "There's always a sale being made."

As a founder, you're always selling. You sell prospects on your service; you sell your team on your systems, culture, and vision; you sell investors on your upside; and one day, you'll sell a buyer on your entire business.

That's why the following applies to you, even if you never knock on a single door.

Photographers rely on shot lists. Teachers prepare lesson plans. Coaches craft game plans. What about elite salespeople? They close like clockwork by following frameworks.

Winners don't wing it. First they prepare. Then they adapt.

Just look at the New England Patriots. During their historic run, Bill Belichick and Tom Brady became legends of preparation. For years, only one sign hung in the team's locker room—a quote from Sun Tzu: "Every battle is won before it is fought." A daily reminder that preparation is everything.

The Patriots never stepped onto the field without a game

plan, but Belichick also trusted Brady to adjust on the fly. The game plan, as Belichick often suggests, is only a starting point.

Sales is no different. A framework is your starting point. Like a shot list, lesson plan, or game plan, it gives every rep both the structure to win and the freedom to adapt in real time.

Here's the exact framework we used to consistently win over even the toughest, most skeptical prospects and achieve a remarkable 85 percent close rate across the board.

## The 50,000 Doors Framework

Over six years, I knocked on upward of 50,000 real doors and just as many imaginary ones. After absorbing thousands of rejections and eventually figuring out how to flip every objection you can imagine, I finally built confidence. Then I built something even better: this universal framework.

This simple five-step framework helped us regularly close even the most ice-cold prospects who would rather listen to a teenager tell them about religion than even make a smidge of eye contact with the friendly neighborhood bug man.

*Connection → Curiosity → Tailored Value → Momentum → Close*

Like the Value Vortex, the genius is in its simplicity.

It's so simple even a 10-year-old can use it. Just ask my nephew Mark. He started knocking on doors with Green Mango as a kid, and today, he's raised over $10 million for the company he works for because he knows how to sell.

It worked for him. It worked for me, the shy kid who would rather keep to himself. It worked for servers-turned-salespeople. It worked for our managers, like Matt, who closed over $1 million in sales in a single year. It worked at the door, online, and everywhere in between with the occasional audible, or detour, sprinkled in as needed.

Whether you're selling prospects, employees, or potential buyers, this framework opens doors and closes deals, period.

Let's break down each step so you know how to properly use it.

## STEP 1: CONNECTION: SHATTER THEIR WALLS WITH COMMON GROUND

Everyone expects the pest control guy to talk about pests, but nobody expects him to comment on your Travis Scotts, ask if you're a collector, and actually sound like a sneakerhead.

At Green Mango, we always talked about the customer first, not their bugs. It's the same move Joe Girard used to sell more cars than anyone in history. The Guinness World Record holder brought up their shoes, their watch, their kids, *then* their car. Evan's not a sports guy, but when he was knocking on doors, he watched just enough SportsCenter to be dangerous. (I didn't believe him, so I tested him...and he passed.)

I've probably closed more deals talking about Little League, dogs, and sand dunes than anything else. That's why we trained our reps to spot everything—the ASU flag hanging by the door, the muddy hiking boots on the porch, the Midwest accent on the other end of the line—in search of one thing: common ground.

Jumping right into your pitch is like trying to bear-hug a stranger on the street. It instantly pushes them away.

Breaking down walls with common ground, on the other hand, works everywhere—whether you're selling pest control, recruiting talent, drumming up buy-in from your team, or winning over buyers.

### *STEP 2: CURIOSITY: THE SMOOTH BRIDGE*

Now that you've built a connection, use your observations to casually lead them toward the problem you solve.

As Brian Tracy often emphasizes, effective selling is based on asking the right questions—not giving the right answers.

I call this the curiosity bridge. It's typically just a quick, natural question or two that ties your intel to your solution without ever feeling like a pitch.

At Green Mango, it sounded like, "Moose is awesome!" (Their big Bernese wagging his tail at the door.) "Your neighbor Kelli over there just called us about scorpions. Have you seen any around?" Or "Looks like your kids practically live in that pool. How have the mosquitoes been lately?"

See the pattern?

Instead of launching right into features, we used *their* world—their family, their home, their needs—to set the table for our pitch.

This principle applies everywhere you're trying to sell anything.

When we installed cameras in our trucks (which could've easily felt a little "Big Brother"-ish to our techs), instead of rattling off specs, I simply asked, "When was the last time you worried about getting blamed for something that wasn't your fault?"

When pitching buyers, a better question might be, "When you're evaluating businesses, do you tend to prioritize EBITDA or top-line revenue?"

Instead of pitching at them, the curiosity bridge sets the table for them to start selling themselves.

### STEP 3: TAILORED VALUE: PERSONALIZATION IS EVERYTHING

Most reps rattle off features like they're reading from a teleprompter. There's zero context or connection. It's like trying to sell snow tires at the sand dunes—wrong offer, wrong place.

Features *tell*. Benefits *sell*. And tailored ones close faster and convert better.

Here's what tailoring actually sounds like: "With our Tri-Bloc technology, we're the only provider in the Valley that guarantees scorpion control, so you don't have to worry about Moose roaming around outside. And if you ever happen to see a scorpion nearby, we'll come back at no charge—no questions asked." (Hint: You won't.)

"All of our premium treatments are safe for pets and people. You won't have to get out of the house or force the kids inside when we come by. In fact, one of our customer's kids even dressed up as a Green Mango tech for Halloween—around here, our techs are like superheroes."

See the difference?

Tailoring proves you were listening and that you care. Whether you're selling to prospects, leading employees, or pitching buyers, the old adage often attributed to Teddy Roosevelt still rings true today: "People don't care how much you know until they know how much you care."

### STEP 4: MOMENTUM: GET THEM EXCITED WITH THE HYPE BUILDER

When you're skiing downhill, the last thing you want to do is stop to re-strap your boots. It kills all your momentum.

Same thing in sales. When they're nodding, lean into it.

Keep the energy flowing and seamlessly advance the sale to the final step with what I call the Hype Builder.

It's a smooth, natural transition that builds excitement without feeling forced. Phrases like "It makes all the difference" or "You're going to love..." are two of my personal favorites.

For example: "Having that scorpion-free guarantee makes all the difference when you've got dogs and kids running around." Or "You're going to love hosting out back without swatting at mosquitoes every five seconds."

To be clear, this isn't just useful for selling prospects.

When we installed those truck cameras, I told our techs, "Knowing you're protected from false claims makes all the difference when accidents happen." When pitching buyers, it might be, "You're going to love having a business that already runs without me."

It's the smooth bridge that keeps you gliding straight across the finish line.


## STEP 5: CLOSE: ASSUME THE SALE BY GIVING THEM OPTIONS

Our sales manual taught reps six different closes, but the Options Close is hands-down my favorite. Instead of asking *if* they want to move forward, you ask *how* they'd like to move forward.

Think about parenting. When Lyss would ask Banks or Ivory, "Do you want to brush your teeth?" she'd get the same answer every time: "No."

Flip it to "Do you want to use the Batman toothbrush or the Mario one?" "Yellow or pink?" and just like that, they'd be scrubbing away.

It's the same in sales.

Instead of, "Do you want to move forward?" you ask, "Does tomorrow morning or afternoon work better for you?" or "Would you like to put that on your Visa or your Mastercard?"

With your team it might sound like "We're scheduling camera installs for Wednesday and Friday. Which works best for you?"

With buyers it's more like "Would you prefer to send over a rough valuation by email or submit an IOI (indication of interest)?"

You're still giving them a choice, but you're removing the only answer that kills the sale: "No."

## The Best Closers Are Built, Not Born

As the story goes, Jerry Seinfeld wrote one joke a day every day for years and tracked it on a calendar so he wouldn't "break the chain." Stephen King famously writes 2,000 words per day. Tiger Woods didn't take days off. His dad once warned him, "You have to be twice as good to be given half a chance." Woods regularly hit balls until his hands bled.

Every elite performer shares one thing: daily, deliberate practice. And in sales, that starts with role-playing.

At Green Mango, daily role-playing was the cornerstone of our sales training. Like Aristotle said, "We are what we repeatedly do. Excellence, then, is not an act, but a habit."

That's what I'm teaching Banks right now. Who do you think is going to become the better basketball player—the kid who gets up 250 shots a day or the kid who fires off 25,000 shots once?

Exactly.

That doesn't mean we mastered every aspect of sales. We didn't. Instead, Dusty and I focused on mastering that framework. By role-playing daily, we built unconscious competence.

Closing became as second nature as riding a bike. Then our reps trained daily to reach that same level.

Start there, but don't stop.

As we grew, we tacked on a rotating six-week training cycle. Later, when we transitioned from doors to phones, we invested in recording every call so our sales managers could break them down like game film.

If you don't have the resources yet, do what I did early on: Record yourself role-playing, then study the tape. It's like working out in front of a mirror to master your form.

Like I said back in Chapter 3: "Train like you fight, fight like you train." A framework without training is like a parachute that's never been packed. It's useless the moment you need it.

## Don't Pay a Lifeguard Like a Navy SEAL

I was recently on a call with one of my private clients, Matt, who owns a fast-growing service company doing a few million bucks in annual revenue.

He and his partner, Chris, had just hired someone he referred to as a "killer inbound sales rep."

"Fifty bucks a sale!" he said proudly.

*Every* sale? I cringed. "That's about 30 bucks too high."

This was compensation for an *inbound* rep, not an *outbound* one. That's the key. Those two roles aren't remotely the same.

The inbound rep is picking up a conversation a prospect asked to have by calling in or filling out a form. In this scenario, the prospect is at least "warm," if not red hot. The outbound rep, on the other hand, must break the ice at the doors or through cold calling.

Paying them the same is like handing a lifeguard and a

Navy SEAL the same paycheck. Sure, they both keep people safe, but only one gets dropped behind enemy lines.

Matt was unknowingly about to pay outbound rates for inbound effort. That simple mistake was on track to cost him up to $500,000 a year. I wasn't trying to burst his bubble—I was trying to save him a fortune. I hope that one call did just that.

Now my hope is that the next few paragraphs do the same for you, because when comp is off, margins, morale, retention, and results all suffer.

## OUTBOUND REPS ARE YOUR SEALS

The best outbound reps want commission, and you should want to give it to them. Commission rewards results, and you can absolutely afford to give them a solid slice of the pie because you only pay when they perform.

When you're bootstrapping—especially in home services—pure commission is as efficient as it gets. There's no salary, benefits, or overhead. Just output. Your outbound reps should get a bigger piece of the pie than your inbound reps because they're creating something (revenue) from nothing.

At Green Mango, we paid our outbound reps around 40 to 65 percent of the contract value they sold. That meant they were banking around $300 on each new customer. The exact percentage depends on your margins, market, and model, but either way it should be significantly more than what your inbound reps get.

## INBOUND REPS ARE YOUR LIFEGUARDS

Inbound leads come *to* your rep from your marketing and advertising. Not only did you spend money to generate them, but they are also far easier to sell than Don at his door or Donna who just happened to answer the phone, because these prospects are already warm.

You don't need sales assassins here. You just need consistent, coachable reps who follow your system with discipline. Thus, these reps often receive closer to five to 15 percent of contract value.

In sales, commission drives performance. Just make sure the size of the reward matches the weight of the work.

## Track the Right Metrics

Most owners think they need more leads, but what they really need is more conversions. That's why close rate is the ultimate performance indicator of your sales success.

At Green Mango, everything we just covered helped us lift our close rate from a meager 33 to a healthy 85 percent. That's the difference between needing 100 leads to make 33 sales and needing just 39.

Which would you prefer?

But just tracking the outcome is not enough. It's like seeing the check engine light come on, then guessing which part to replace. Without diagnostics, you're just throwing parts at the problem.

To fix what's actually broken and keep things running smoothly, you've got to pop the hood. That's why we tracked three diagnostic metrics alongside close rate. With them, we could pinpoint exactly where deals were slipping and where we could improve. I can't stress enough how important it is that you track the following diagnostic metrics too:

1. **Contact rate** – How many leads are you actually getting in touch with? We always aimed for north

of 75 percent, but anything above 65 percent is reasonable. If your contact rate is lower, you likely have a speed or responsiveness issue.

2. **Contact-to-close rate** – Of the people you talk to, how many are you closing? Our goal was to stay above 90 percent. Anything below that and your framework, scripts, or training likely need work.

3. **Close-to-service rate** – Of the customers you close, what percentage are being scheduled and serviced? Anything below 98 percent is a massive miss. If this number's off, your handoff is broken and you're leaking revenue.

You see, we used to treat "closed" as "done." Big mistake. We'd done the hard part (selling them), only to let customers slip through the cracks at handoff. Eventually, we fixed it by building a system to immediately push every sale into scheduling. Then we tracked our close-to-service rate and watched our revenue rise.

With full visibility into the pipeline, we could fine-tune every step to run more smoothly and convert higher. That visibility helped us fix what was broken and optimize what wasn't.

In short, it turned our sales pipeline into a well-oiled machine. As that got dialed in, we could take things a step further, and so can you.

With that in mind, let's get into Step 2: Duplicate, where we automatically turn one customer into two.

## STEP 2: DUPLICATE EVERY CUSTOMER

What if, after closing one customer, you could just press the "copy" button on a machine and watch new customers print out automatically?

That's sort of what we did at Green Mango, simply by asking for referrals at point of sale. Every day, you refer things without even thinking about it: shows, restaurants, books, you name it. Referring is second nature. Why not ask for what people already do?

Asking for referrals is so simple a child can do it, and the results are staggering. Even when we spent over $1 million a year on marketing and advertising (more on that in the next chapter), guess what outperformed it all?

Referrals. And it wasn't even close.

For every customer we paid to acquire through advertising, our referral program brought in two more—without the marketing spend.

Would you rather spend millions on ads or let your customers do the selling *for* you?

For all the things we did wrong over the years, asking for

referrals at the point of sale was one thing we got right from the very beginning, back when we began knocking on doors in our very first neighborhood, which ironically was called Cameron Ranch.

## Referrals Are the Eighth Wonder of the Business World

Einstein reportedly called compound interest "the eighth wonder of the world."

Why?

Interest earns interest, quietly building fortunes over time. Referrals work the same way. Every customer who refers becomes another customer who refers, creating customers who create customers.

But it doesn't stop there.

### REFERRED CUSTOMERS ARE THE BEST CUSTOMERS

At Green Mango, the average customer stayed with us 3.7 years. A referred customer, however, stuck with us for an average of 5.2 years. That's a full year and a half longer.

For us, that was an average of nine additional bimonthly treatments. Think of those nine visits like a free license to print money, stacking revenue with zero additional acquisition costs.

Coconut Cleaning saw the same effect.

The average new customer spent about $450 on their first job ticket. Compare that to a referred customer who, on average, spent up to $720 from the get-go.

That's 60 percent more revenue, per customer, from the jump.

For those reasons (and more), I consider referrals the eighth wonder of the business world.

This isn't just a home service thing either.

My friend, photographer Ben Christensen, got his start shooting weddings. Wedding photography is often known for long hours, demanding clients, and, at times, modest pay. At one reception, he met a couple who worked for Nike. The next thing he knew, he was shooting events for the sportswear giant.

Today, Ben's portfolio includes Disney World, Boot Barn, and Columbia.

One relationship opened doors that advertising never could because referrals scale trust in a way money simply can't.

Yet most entrepreneurs undervalue referrals and overvalue marketing and advertising. They treat referrals like an afterthought, and by doing so, they never get results that remotely compare to what we did.

Let me show you how to build a referral machine that duplicates your customer base and has the power to pack a stadium with raving fans.

## How to Build Your Own Referral Machine

When we tallied the numbers leading up to our acquisition, the results were mind-boggling: more than 25,000 referred customers in Green Mango's lifetime.

The Footprint Center in Phoenix, where the Phoenix Suns play, holds 18,000 people. Picture an NBA arena filled to the brim, then add another 7,000 people spilling into the streets outside, begging to get in.

That's how many referrals we converted. We could have packed a stadium *and* the street out front.

It gets even crazier. Each of those customers spent upward of $2,835 with us over time (that's about $135 per quarter for 5.2 years of our primary service, what we call General Pest

Control). Do the math: 25,000 customers × $2,835 = $70,875,000 in revenue.

While those numbers are phenomenal, what I'm most proud of is that we built something people were genuinely excited to talk about.

But here's the thing: It didn't happen *just* because we asked. Most business owners learn that the hard way.

Want referrals? You've got to earn them. Here's how we earned $70 million worth of them—and how you can, too.

## STEP 1: DELIVER A REFERRAL-WORTHY EXPERIENCE

Referrals are earned, not given. Strive to be so good, customers would feel *guilty* not telling their friends.

At Green Mango, that was the goal.

We trained our techs to overdeliver, we showed up when we said we would, and we guaranteed results. In other words, we did the exact opposite of what people expected from a pest control provider.

Were we perfect? Not even close. When we messed up, we owned it—fast—and made it right. That's the kind of experience that makes someone say, "You have to try these guys."

We'll get into specific ways to overdeliver in Chapter 7, but for now, just remember: You can't out-market a poor experience.

## STEP 2: ALWAYS OFFER TWO-WAY INCENTIVES

Most businesses make the mistake of only rewarding the new customer. That's like giving all the credit to the guest and none to the host. Why would the host ever throw another party?

The best referral programs reward both the referrer and the

referred. When both people benefit, you double their motivation to pay, stay, and refer.

At Green Mango, we kept it simple: "Refer a friend, and you'll both get a free service."

## STEP 3: DANGLE CUSTOM CARROTS

If you want more referrals, give people more to talk about.

Referral campaigns are like sales spiffs for your customers. They add urgency, bigger prizes, and more buzz.

We once gave away a three-night stay at Great Wolf Lodge. We straight-up told customers these were bribes in our emails: "To make it easier than ever to spread the word about the Valley's best pest control, this month only—we're giving away free pest control for a year."

The more friends you referred, the more chances you had to win.

At Coconut, we sent customers to Hawaii on our dime. At Agave, we gave away Stanley water bottles and Apple AirPods Max. One year, we even gave away a truck. Just like the tailored incentives or "carrots" we talked about in the previous chapter, every incentive was tailored to what our customers actually wanted.

Green Mango and Coconut primarily served families, so vacations were a hit. Agave's younger, single, on-the-go customers were pumped about the gear (and the vehicle).

The goal was always the same: Stack the incentives, increase urgency, and flood the business with referrals.

## STEP 4: KNOW YOUR NUMBERS

We always gave referred customers a free initial service valued at $199, which later increased to $299. We also covered the referring customer's next service visit, which was typically about a $135 value.

That's up to $434 invested in each referral relationship.

Other business owners looked at me cross-eyed, convinced we were crazy. "You're giving away too much," they'd say. "You're cutting into your margins, right?"

Wrong.

Who wouldn't trade $434 for $2,835?

That's what our average *referred* customer spent over their lifetime with us. Thus, that $434 investment represented just 15 percent of their total LTV, or lifetime value (we'll go deeper on LTV shortly).

We made almost $7 in revenue for every $1 we gave away. That's why we could afford to give so much more than everyone else and pack our schedule with referred customers.

Point is, we knew our numbers. Do you?

You might be surprised by how much you can afford to give. And the more you give, the more you get.

## STEP 5: MAKE IT SHOCKINGLY EASY TO REFER FRIENDS

Your goal should be to make referring a friend as easy as using Venmo, requesting an Uber, or ordering on Amazon.

A referral program with friction is like inviting someone to a party but making them solve a puzzle to get the address. Most people will just stay home.

That's why you want to make referring a piece of cake. The easier, the better.

Mark Zuckerberg once said, "A trusted referral is the Holy Grail of advertising."

When Weston, a business owner in my 1% Club, reviewed his March numbers after four years in business (and just one month in the Club), he had huge news to share with the group: His revenue had just soared a whopping 24 percent month over month.

What changed?

He increased prices *and* started a referral program.

Referred customers come to you pre-sold, pre-qualified, and predisposed to trust you. That's why they spend more money, spend more often, and stay longer, all while bringing their own friends along. Isn't that what you want every customer to do? That's how revenue multiplies. With that, let's jump into Step 3: Multiply, so I can show you how to make every customer worth more.

# STEP 3: MULTIPLY CUSTOMER VALUE

Starbucks earns an estimated $14,099 from every $5 cup of coffee they sell to a new customer.

Meanwhile, many businesses operate backward. They spend their version of $14,099 just to close a $5 customer. Simply put, they pour money into acquisition before making every customer they've already acquired worth more money.

What if you could make every two customers worth four?

That's where customer lifetime value (LTV) comes in. LTV is the total revenue a customer brings to your business over the course of your relationship. Raise your LTV, and you raise your profits and your multiple at the same time.

Say it costs you $10 between marketing and sales to acquire one customer. If that customer is worth $100, you make $90 in profit. If that customer is worth $1,000, you make $990 in profit.

It's the same $10 spent, but it's 10 times the return thanks to a higher LTV. The way I see it, it's like making one customer worth 10.

And it gets even better.

You can then use that $990 in extra margin to acquire 99 more customers at $10 apiece, without pulling another dollar out of your pocket. After covering acquisition costs, and by multiplying LTV, you're left with $98,010 in profit.

That's multiplication.

The higher your LTV, the faster and cheaper you can grow. Plus, buyers take notice because they care about quality *and* quantity. They told me so. LTV is the ultimate sign of customer quality. That's why buyers zeroed in on our LTV the moment we went to market.

So how do you maximize LTV so you can make one customer worth 10?

Simple.

Here are the three key levers to pull:

1. Get customers to spend more up front.
2. Get customers to buy more often.
3. Get customers to stay longer.

Though this is typically a combined effort between sales and marketing (more on marketing in the next chapter), let's break each one down now.


## Lever 1: Get Customers to Spend More *Up Front*

Once someone says yes, they're primed to say yes again.

That's why smart companies stack purchases with upsells and add-ons at the point of sale.

It's no different than Costco having you buy in bulk. You can buy 12 rolls of Charmin or load up on 30 rolls of Kirkland. Why not pay a little more to "save" a little more? You feel like you scored a deal, and Costco multiplied your value six seconds after you flashed your membership card for the first time.

Upsells are Costco's bread and butter. Subscriptions were ours.

At Green Mango, we didn't sell pest control as a one-time service; we required most customers to commit to a year up front, with billing set quarterly. It was like closing four sales at once.

I'm convinced subscriptions can work for any service business. Competitors looked at us like we had three heads each when we rolled out a subscription program for Coconut Cleaning, and I get it. To my knowledge, subscriptions had never been done, or at least done well, in residential cleaning.

The norm was to see customers once every 18 months or so. That's one sale every 18 months. It's tough to build a valuable business when it rarely sees its customers.

So we created The Coconut Club, a membership that gave customers special incentives to commit to quarterly cleanings. Their carpets stayed fresher, their homes looked cleaner, spots and stains were erased immediately, and we started seeing them four times a year instead of once every year and a half. That's six times more than before, essentially multiplying their LTV by six at the point of sale.

If I were a photographer, a barber, or anything similar, I'd be offering subscriptions yesterday. It baffles me that most don't. Another way to get customers to spend more up front is to let them sample your products and services.

Costco hands you a taste of something you didn't know you needed until you tried it. Next thing you know, you're throwing a 48-pack of frozen taquitos into your cart.

Coconut Cleaning's version of samples is demos. On carpet cleaning jobs, techs would vacuum a small section of the customer's couch with a clean white cloth attached to the hose.

What was once pure white now looked like it had been dragged through the desert: streaked with brown, coated with dust, and stained with grime.

Stunned, customers regularly added a full couch cleaning to their carpet cleaning bill on the spot, happily spending another $250 they hadn't planned on.

One minute you're getting your carpets cleaned, the next, it's your furniture too. It's much the same as when you walk into Costco for toilet paper and leave with a three-pack of Vitamix bottles, a rotisserie chicken, and a kayak.

However you do it—whether you close a subscription at point of sale, cross-sell, bundle, upsell, sample, or demo— getting customers to spend more up front multiplies LTV from the jump.

## Lever 2: Get Customers to Spend More Often

Frequency matters.

In some businesses, like ours, the customer's initial purchase is a subscription. In others, it's the second lever pulled after the first sale.

Either way, you're getting customers to commit to spending more from the outset or spending more often. Aside from their initial subscription, we got our general pest control (GPC) customers to spend more often by stacking subscriptions with specialty services like mosquito misting, termite prevention, weed removal, and more.

We promoted those specialty services when specific pest activity was high: mosquito treatments after heavy monsoon rains, rodent prevention when temperatures dropped, weed control in early spring, and snake prevention before the desert heat rolled in.

Take snake prevention, our most affordable specialty

service. Customers paid an $80 initial setup fee, then an additional $29 each quarter for maintenance and monitoring. It might not sound like much, but when you stack it across just 1,000 customers, you're talking $80,000 in setup fees up front, plus another $29,000 in recurring revenue every quarter. All that, simply because they're spending more often.

Plus, Green Mango customers enrolled in two or more services were 93 percent less likely to cancel with us *and* they stuck with us for an average of *11.7 years*.

Our approach was no different than Costco luring you back in with pumpkin pies in November, Christmas trees in December, or patio sets and backyard pools in May. It's all part of what Costco cofounder James Sinegal called their "treasure-hunt atmosphere": Come back often, because you never know what you'll find.

Coconut Cleaning followed a similar playbook with back-to-school carpet refreshes, spring cleaning campaigns, holiday discounts before Thanksgiving and Christmas, and more.

Specialty services, weather, holidays, seasons—they're all fantastic ways to get customers to spend more often.

## Lever 3: Get Customers to Spend Longer

The longer they stay, the more they pay.

But what happens when things inevitably go sideways? When a tech shows up 20 minutes late, when ants return with a vengeance, when there's an issue of any kind? Do you even notice? Does your team point to the door? I see it all the time. You work hard to get customers in the front door only to leave the back door wide open.

We slammed it shut by building a ladder—a retention ladder—where every rung delivered more value than the last.

## RUNG 1: LISTEN

That's it. Genuinely listen. It's like Walmart founder Sam Walton said, "If you don't listen to your customers, someone else will." You'd be amazed at how many upset customers simply want to be heard.

Listening works like a pressure valve: Let them vent, blow off steam, and feel heard so that they don't explode. It seems small, but a few quick minutes of undivided attention could save you thousands of dollars. It's a no-cost way to keep customers.

## RUNG 2: GIVE VALUE THAT COSTS YOU NOTHING

When listening wasn't enough, we climbed to the second rung, where giving real value costs you nothing but feels like everything to the customer.

Remember those high school fundraiser cards? The ones packed with free car washes, pizza deals, and ice cream cones, and somehow worth $500 in value for just $20?

We created our own.

I partnered with top local service pros and bundled their best offers into a retention package no competitor could touch. Every card included things our customers would actually use, like a free oil change, HVAC tune-up, carpet cleaning from Coconut, and more.

It took legwork, but it was worth it. While others were offering 10 percent off, we handed customers over $2,000 in real value—presented on a professionally designed card with a private QR code that felt exclusive every step of the way.

*RUNG 3: EMPOWER YOUR TEAM TO MAKE IT RIGHT*

If need be, we climbed to the third and final rung, inspired by Ritz-Carlton.

The Ritz's famous $2,000 rule empowers employees to spend up to $2,000 per guest, per incident, without manager approval. That means any employee can offer a comped room, a free meal, upgraded service, or another gesture to solve a guest's problems and keep them happy.

We modeled that.

In addition to the $2,000 "Varsity Card" I just mentioned, our managers were empowered to offer up to $500 in freebies to disgruntled customers, on Green Mango's tab.

If we showed up late for a service call, we could comp it 100 percent. If we missed a spot and pests returned, we'd not only re-treat for free, but we could also offer to cover their next treatment at no charge. If a tech damaged something on the property, the repair was on us and done immediately (we actually kept a handyman on standby just in case).

For us, $500 was a drop in the ocean. When every customer is worth thousands per year between GPC and specialty services, spending up to $500 to keep them happy is easy math. What's more, every manager knew of this $500 rule and felt empowered to apply it.

What are you doing to keep customers spending longer? To close the back door? Are you actively listening to their concerns, or are they screaming into a void?

What can you give them that creates so much value, switching to a competitor seems silly? What specific dollar amount are your managers authorized to spend to save a customer? How fast can your team turn an issue into an opportunity?

Just like you offer customers incentives to join, give them

reasons to stay so that they keep spending. Build your retention ladder today.


### The Compound Effect of Lever Stacking

One lever is good. Two is better. Three is best.

At Green Mango, we basically pulled all three at once.

Subscriptions meant customers committed to spending more up front. Specialty services meant they spent more often. And with our retention efforts, they kept spending year after year.

When you get customers to spend more up front, more often, and for longer, you create a compound effect that transforms your entire business by turning one sale into four, four into eight, and eight into 16. That's the power of stacking levers.


## Nobody Buys a Business Without Customers

Start by closing one customer at a time with the 50,000 Doors Framework. Double up on every customer by duplicating them through referrals. Then multiply their value by pulling all three levers until one customer is worth 16.

Close. Duplicate. Multiply. That's the formula for building to sell.

# SALES PRO TIPS: THE FORTUNE'S IN THE FOLLOW-THROUGH

Before we wrap up, here are a few quick-hitting sales pro tips that made a huge difference for us—and can do the same for you.

## Bill Before You Fulfill

Amazon collects payment before shipping, grocery stores scan items before you leave, and restaurants expect payment before you walk out the door. Your business should be no different. When you're bootstrapping like we were at the beginning, you need today's payment to fund tomorrow's fulfillment (to pay your techs, buy supplies, and keep the lights on). Always bill before you fulfill. A customer who balks at paying up front is often a customer who wasn't planning to pay at all.

## Front-Load Value (and Revenue)

As I mentioned, we charged more for our initial service visit than subsequent visits, and we did it on purpose. First, it covered the heavier workload required on our first visit as we performed both a full pest inspection and a comprehensive flush-out. Second, it accelerated cash flow, helping us cover acquisition costs faster while creating a cushion during tougher months with extra pay periods or higher PTO. Third, as LTV multiplied, it became a powerful sales tool. We could offer discounts or even free initials from time to time, knowing we were trading short-term pain for long-term gain. Whenever possible, look for smart ways to front-load value.

## Not All Customers Are Created Equal

Customer quality matters. Customers acquired through cold outreach, like door-to-door or cold calling, tend to leave first and spend less. Think about it: You (literally) just talked them into joining. That's why I always tell business owners to treat outbound sales like a shot in the arm or a stepping stone. It's great for jump-starting your customer base, but it's not a long-term strategy.

# FROM SELLING TO SCALING

Once you can sell consistently and predictably, you've earned the right to scale faster.

That's where marketing comes in. If sales is the spark, marketing is the fuel.

## Chapter Summary

- Close. Duplicate. Multiply. Sales is about turning one customer into 16.
- Skyrocket close rates with the 50,000 Doors Framework: Connection → Curiosity → Tailored Value → Momentum → Close
- Practice until it's second nature. Role-play daily. Drill like it's game day. Never "break the chain."
- Outbound reps should earn a larger share of each contract since they're closing *cold* prospects. Inbound reps should earn less since they're closing *warm* leads.

- Track these diagnostic metrics alongside close rate: contact rate (aim for 65 percent+), contact-to-close rate (aim for 90 percent+), and close-to-service rate (aim for 98 percent+).
- Referred customers are the best customers. Deliver a referral-worthy customer experience, offer incentives worth talking about, and always ask at the point of sale.
- Multiply LTV by pulling three levers:
    - Get customers to spend more up front (subscriptions, upsells, demos)
    - Get them to buy more often (seasonal offers, specialty services)
    - Get them to stay longer (retention ladder: listen, add value, empower your team)

# SIX
# MARKETING



*"In marketing, I've seen only one strategy that can't miss—and that is to market to your best customers first, your best prospects second, and the rest of the world last."*
–John Romero

The crowd lining both sides of the street started buzzing. First, murmurs. Then laughter. Fingers pointed. Phones shot up.

Then, through the sea of running shoes and race bibs at the 2010 New York City Marathon, something emerged.

A bright blue, life-sized object bobbed and swayed with each step, arms poking out from the sides and a curly-haired head popping out of the spout on top. Everyone cheered as the bizarre spectacle lumbered past, a human juice box with four massive letters stretched across the front in bold white font: ZICO.

What occurred on New York City's First Avenue that day was a marketing masterclass from Jesse Itzler, a partner responsible for bringing ZICO coconut water to America.

In 2010, coconut water was virtually unknown to most Americans. There was no established market, as behemoths like Gatorade had been dominating the hydration space for decades.

"When we started ZICO, we had no money to market," the curly-haired Itzler later explained. "We wrote down 50 ideas of things we could do to get attention and press on a bootstrapped budget."

That list led to Itzler and six buddies securing marathon bibs and transforming themselves into human Tetra Paks for the race. While Gatorade spent millions to be an official sponsor that day, ZICO spent a few bucks—and stole the show.

"We were loud...we handed out product...we talked to everybody on the course during the race," Itzler recalled. For a product few Americans had ever heard of, it was 26.2 miles of dirt-cheap marketing that worked like a charm. ZICO, unsurprisingly, was built to sell. Just three years later, Coca-Cola fully acquired it.

Now picture this: the Arizona Home and Garden Show at Cardinals Stadium. 25,000 people streaming through the doors, wandering past rows of booths selling everything from solar panels to kitchen renovations.

Every booth handing out the same candy and business cards. Everyone blending in. Forgotten by dinner.

Until a crowd forms around a gleaming Lamborghini SVJ. The $700,000 supercar is magnetic, its exotic presence completely out of place among the practical home improvement displays. Two words stretch across the doors: *Green Mango*.

Everyone wants to know more.

Nearby, a Rolls Royce sits regally wrapped in Coconut Cleaning's soft blue branding, creating another island of excitement in the sea of sameness.

It was a spectacle as disruptive as a Bengal tiger in a petting zoo. And guess what?

It worked.

Ours were the only booths that I guarantee almost every one of those 25,000 people never forgot.

Like Itzler's juice box stunt, we didn't have the most money, but we drew the most attention. The trick was, we didn't *buy* those cars. We *rented* them. Then we paid next to nothing to have them wrapped with our logos for the day.

That one bold move reframed pest control and carpet cleaning from chores to luxury, from forgettable to photo-worthy, from ordinary services to something premium, exciting, even status-worthy.

More, it was just a start, which leads me to rule number one of five that we learned while scaling Green Mango through marketing and sales.

Green Mango Lamborghini

# RULE 1: START SOMEWHERE (NOT EVERYWHERE)

Start small. Start weird. Start memorable. Just start somewhere.

That doesn't mean it has to be a Lambo. Maybe it's a $10 boosted Facebook post, a clever Google ad, or just showing up consistently in local community groups.

The best marketing move is the one you'll actually make.

In our case, closing customers one by one at their front doors gave us the cash flow to fund our marketing efforts. Those sales dollars paid for marketing and advertising, which generated more leads, which fueled more sales.

That flywheel is how we grew from banging on doors to cruising past our very own billboards on the highway, and from seven figures in annual revenue to eight.

In other words, sales funded marketing and marketing scaled sales.

Some business owners either try to market too early, too big, or too broad. Others never start at all. They get stuck waiting for the perfect idea, the perfect plan, or the perfect budget.

But if you can't close, every marketing dollar becomes a

wasted one. Instead of an investment, your marketing efforts are a donation. Even if you can close, if you're spending $14,000 to attract customers who spend $5, the math doesn't math.

My point is, marketing doesn't mean advertising across 10 channels at once. It means starting somewhere, with one move that makes the biggest splash.

Think Itzler's human juice box, our Lamborghini, and Coconut's Rolls Royce.

When budgets are tight, creativity is your capital. If you can't outspend your competition, how can you outshine them? How can you deliver Gatorade-level impact on a ZICO budget?

Consider starting with a list of 50 ideas, like Itzler. How can you generate buzz? Stop people in their tracks? Do more with less?

There's no perfect recipe for marketing. What worked for ZICO probably wouldn't work for Coke. Heck, what worked for Green Mango didn't always work for Coconut. However, there is a universal truth: As Zig Ziglar put it, "You don't have to be great to start, but you have to start to be great."

So...start.

# RULE 2: AIM FOR YOUR SUPERCONSUMER

When we first ran radio ads on 104.7's *Johnjay & Rich Show*, leads rolled in, our customer acquisition cost (CAC) stayed lean, and everything felt dialed. So we doubled down. We invested in more radio, expecting twice the leads for twice the spend. Instead, lead volume tanked by more than half.

What happened?

The same ads flopped on a different station because they reached a different listener. 104.7 attracted suburban moms and East Valley homeowners, our superconsumers. 102.5, a country station, skewed rural. One audience wanted premium pest control and would happily pay for it; the other was more likely to handle it themselves.

Now, I'm not saying you should go run a bunch of radio ads. That's not the point. Radio was just one of many channels we tested over the years, and it's one of many that we maximized as we got to know our superconsumers like the back of our hand.

Do you know yours?

If you don't, you could double your spend and end up with

half the leads. That's exactly what many service owners do. They spend more instead of spending smarter.

Aiming for your superconsumers is the key to spending smarter. It's the difference between going wide and going deep. In my experience, going deep is the secret to scaling both your marketing spend and your business.

But before you can go deeper, you have to know who your superconsumer is.

Superconsumers are the top 10 percent of your customer base. They're the ones who pay, stay, and refer. As Eddie Yoon explained in *Harvard Business Review*, across virtually every category—from Velveeta cheese to air travel—10 percent of consumers account for more than 50 percent of profits. The same is true in service businesses.

Imagine what focusing your marketing entirely on that 10 percent could do for your bottom line, your referrals, your reviews, your team's morale, your valuation, and more.

Once we identified our superconsumers—affluent home-owners in Scottsdale, Queen Creek, and Gilbert with spouses, kids, pets, and a college education—we adjusted our aim. We flyered the right neighborhoods instead of blanketing the entire Valley. We ran geo-targeted ads instead of wasting money on broad, untargeted campaigns. We tailored our messaging to focus on what our superconsumers really wanted: premium protection for the entire family, lasting peace of mind, and professional technicians who show up on time, refuse to cut corners, and treat the customer's home and family like their own.

Suddenly, the same marketing dollars produced outsized returns.

Red Bull took the same approach. Rather than chasing soccer moms or corporate stiffs when they burst onto the scene, they went straight for college students up late studying, partying, or both. Coconut Cleaning, on the other hand, didn't chase broke college kids who just wanted a Swiffer and their deposit back. Instead, we marketed to busy moms in upscale neighborhoods, the ones who cared deeply about a clean, calm, chaos-free home.

Our Instagram reels featured satisfying before-and-afters, our emails had subject lines like "5 things every supermom needs this back-to-school season," we partnered with the local school districts, and we even sponsored community events. In short, we showed up in the right places, with the right message, for the right people—and because of this, business boomed.

Whether you're in pest control, carpet cleaning, or any home service, the playbook is the same: Zero in on your superconsumer. Here's how.

First, mine your customer base for the top 10 percent. Who pays the most, stays the longest, and refers the most often? If you've been in business for years, prioritize LTV. If you're newer, consider leaning on job value or profit.

Then ask yourself, "What do they have in common?"

Start with basic demographics like age, income, location, and marital status, and look for patterns, as overlapping demographics reveal *where* to market to your superconsumer.

Next, consider their psychographics. I always look for three things here:

1. What do they want (their desires)?
2. When do they want it (trigger moments)?
3. What do they fear (their objections)?

Demographics tell you *where* to market; psychographics tell you *what* to say. They often reveal the exact words to use in your ads, emails, sales scripts, and campaigns to attract and convert more superconsumers.

Scaling your marketing doesn't mean casting a wider net. It means fishing in the right waters.

So dive into your data. Identify your superconsumers. Understand their demographics and psychographics inside-out. Then ruthlessly focus your marketing efforts on meeting them where they are and speaking their language.

That's how you'll cut through the noise, stretch your marketing dollars, and scale with speed.

# RULE 3: BRAND BEFORE YOU EXPAND

Dusty was obsessed with branding, and for years, we butted heads over it. I remember we'd be down to our last $3,000 and he'd insist on spending $2,500 on rims. "Branding," he'd say with a shrug.

*Stupid*, I thought.

Why not put that money toward advertising? Acquire more leads, convert them into more customers, make more money, then get your rims?

Dusty was relentless about branding first. I learned over time that he was absolutely right. Branding creates consistency, and without consistency, your marketing efforts will flop.

## Marketing's Rule of 7

Imagine reading a book where every third page switches to a completely different font and writing style. Surely you'd get lost, annoyed, and confused.

David Ogilvy, often called the father of modern advertising, is widely credited with saying, "A confused mind never buys."

That's what you do when you spread an inconsistent message across different channels. You confuse your prospects so much, they never become customers.

This is backed by what I call Marketing's Rule of 7. Research shows consumers need at least *seven* interactions with your brand before they act. What do you think happens when every interaction is completely different?

It's like meeting someone in a suit for a business pitch, then seeing them the next day in a clown costume asking for money. Even if it's the same person, the trust is broken and the sale is dead.

Branding creates consistency. Consistency builds familiarity. And familiarity leads to trust, the very thing you need to attract leads and transform them into customers.

So yeah, start somewhere, but before you go everywhere, make sure your message is dialed in. I'm talking your logo, your colors, your voice, and your visuals. Be consistent across the board, even if it means spending $2,500 on your version of rims.

It's worth it.

# RULE 4: TRACK YOUR CAC BY CHANNEL

When we first launched Green Mango, we had no marketing budget, so we had to sell our way into existence one door at a time. But to scale, we had to master marketing.

Just like in sales, when marketing, guessing isn't good enough. We needed a system, a way to know exactly where every dollar we could measure was going and what we were getting back.

Some marketing channels are not measurable. For example, it's hard to know how many customers a billboard produces without some seriously sophisticated tracking. So at this point, let's split marketing into two parts: advertising and everything else.

Advertising is the part of marketing you can measure, and it's typically focused on attracting new leads. I'm going to leave it at that to keep things moving.

Would you rather buy a business where the owner *feels* like their advertising is working or one where the owner can prove, with hard numbers, exactly how efficiently they can deploy capital to grow? Moreover, which business would you rather *run?*

Buyers want proof, not hunches—and you should, too.

That's where CAC comes in.

In the previous chapter, we talked about making every customer worth more by multiplying LTV. Well, CAC is the other side of that equation. It factors in every cost to close a sale, including marketing and advertising costs (the ones you can track).

Advertising is more math than magic. Done well, you put a nickel into the channel of your choice (like Facebook, Google, or YouTube) and get a quarter out.

But what if you don't know how much you're putting in? What if you're spending a dollar for every quarter? And what if you're spending another dollar to keep that quarter?

That's exactly what happens when you ignore CAC, the one metric that tells you if your advertising is worth it.

Sure, many business owners know their total marketing and advertising budget, and some might even have a gut feel for which channels are working. "We crush it on Facebook," they'll say proudly.

But ask them what their CAC is, and they blink, stare, shrug, and eventually ask, "What's a cack?" To them, it sounds like something a cat does when coughing up a furball...not a metric as vital to your business as LTV.

I've had exchanges like that more times than I can count. I've been on both sides of them because I used to be that guy celebrating leads without considering the acquisition costs—until I found out that not knowing your CAC is like driving with your eyes closed. You might stay on the road for a while, but eventually, you'll crash. When you do, it could wreck everything you've built.

The most important thing to remember is that there is no

business without a customer. The second most important thing to remember is that every customer has an acquisition cost and a lifetime value.

CAC tells you exactly where to spend *and* where to stop. It tells you which channels are printing money as you expand and which ones are lighting it on fire.

Would you rather pay $10 per lead you close or $100? Would you rather close 100 leads for $1,000—or just 10?

If you're not tracking CAC by channel, you'll never know. You'll guess, you'll gamble, and you'll overspend without realizing it. That's how businesses bleed dry without ever seeing the wound.

Here's the good news: Tracking CAC is simple.

*Total marketing spend ÷ number of new customers = CAC*

Spend $1,000 on Google Ads and get 10 customers? Your CAC is $100.

Spend $1,000 and get 100 customers? Your CAC is $10.

Same budget, radically different results.

The key is to track CAC by channel.

Now here's the bigger picture: LTV gives you *quality*. CAC gives you *quantity*.

If your CAC is too high, you bleed to death. If your LTV is too low, you starve to death.

Remember MoviePass? The $10-a-month "unicorn" that flamed out spectacularly? In essence, their CAC was higher than their LTV, and within two years, they crashed and burned.

Meanwhile, Netflix did the opposite. They scaled carefully. Controlled their CAC. Invested in original content to drive up LTV. Today, one is a global powerhouse, and the other is not.

Would you rather build MoviePass or Netflix?

Your goal is simple: Drive CAC down and LTV up.

Imagine two lines on a graph: one going up (LTV), one going down (CAC). The bigger the wedge between them, the faster your profits multiply and the more valuable your business becomes.

That's the real secret to scaling.

When you know exactly what every customer costs and exactly what every customer returns, you don't just grow faster; you grow stronger, you grow smarter, and you build a business buyers fight to own.

That's the difference between businesses that burn out and businesses that break records.

# RULE 5: TRIPLE DOWN ON WHAT WORKS

Once you know your CAC (and LTV), the path forward becomes clear: Eliminate what's not working and triple down on what is, or as Gary Vaynerchuk says, "Stop focusing on what you're bad at. Triple down on what you're great at."

Now here's the nuance: Even the best channels don't scale infinitely. Eventually, you hit diminishing returns where each additional advertising dollar spent delivers less impact than before.

This is why tracking CAC and LTV matters. As channels stop performing like they used to, costs rise and efficiency drops. The businesses that pivot at the right moment stay profitable. Those that don't burn cash on a channel that's no longer working.

By tracking CAC and LTV, you'll know exactly when to pivot before your returns shrink. Track. Pivot. Scale. That's the game.

Now that you know how to acquire customers efficiently, let's talk about how to make every customer worth more by using marketing to drive sales.

# BONUS: DRIP TO DRIVE LTV

As we closed the leads our advertising brought in, our post-sale marketing efforts took over to multiply customer LTV.

The most effective way we did this was with what marketers call drip campaigns, or automated sequences or series of emails (and texts) to get new customers to spend more at the click of a button.

Drip campaigns helped us pull the same three LTV-multiplying levers I mentioned in the last chapter, on demand.

Here's a glimpse at how we did it:

## Lever 1: Spend More Up Front

Our "Welcome Series" highlighted specialty services right away, stacking revenue while excitement (and attention) were at their peak. As mentioned earlier, we also asked for referrals right out of the gate.

## Lever 2: Spend More Often

Seasonal drip campaigns promoted our specialty services at the perfect time. In the spring, we'd promote scorpion control just as temperatures and activity went up. During monsoon season, we'd highlight mosquito abatement. In winter, we'd promote rodent proofing as cold weather drove rats, mice, and gophers indoors.

Flash sales gave us another way to boost frequency. At Coconut, bookings skyrocketed during the holiday season when we offered carpet cleaning discounts just in time for Thanksgiving and Christmas parties. We also saw a surge as the new school year approached, when parents wanted the house clean and calm again. We even tied campaigns to flu season, offering discounts on air duct deep-cleans to help fight cold symptoms.

## Lever 3: Spend Longer

Ongoing engagement (or "value") emails built loyalty, reinforced value, and kept us top of mind, so customers stuck around for years. Topics like "Telltale signs of rodents most homeowners miss" and "Surprising signs of termite damage" kept customers engaged and informed while subtly promoting our specialty services. On top of that, seasonal campaigns and giveaways tied to holidays like Halloween or New Year's Day kept things fresh and timely.

## MARKETING SCALES SALES

Nobody buys a business that can't scale. Start somewhere. Be strategic. Stay consistent. Track your CAC. Triple down on what works. Then drip to drive LTV through the roof so you earn even more from every customer you acquire.

You can sell without marketing, you can market without sales, but you'll never scale without both.

# MARKETING PRO TIPS: SPENDING EVEN SMARTER

Marketing and advertising cost money. Here are a few more tips for spending wisely.

## Track Your CAC and Your Referral Acquisition Cost (RAC)

As I mentioned in the previous chapter, referred customers tend to be your most valuable customers—they convert faster, spend more, stick around longer, and refer others. Treat them that way. In other words, track your RAC, too. If your referred customers are as valuable as ours were, it might make sense to spend even more than you would on other channels to acquire them.

## Give So Much It Hurts (Then Track the Return)

One of my favorite marketing campaigns we ever ran, and one of our most successful, was our "Summer Switchover" campaign. We gave away $2,000 in local bonuses, lululemon gift cards, $5,000 in cash, and a literal helicopter ride to incentivize prospects to switch from their current pest control provider to us. It worked like a charm because we offered so much. And we could only afford to do that because we knew our CAC and LTV like the back of our hand.

## Spend Like the Business You Want To Become

Wondering how much to spend on marketing and advertising? Here's my general rule of thumb:

- For stability, invest 10 to 12 percent of your revenue in marketing.
- For growth, go 17 to 20 percent.
- For market dominance, spend 20 percent of your *desired* revenue.

Yes, it might feel scary to spend that much until you remember that every dollar invested with a clear CAC and solid LTV is fuel, not fire. As long as you know your numbers, spend like the business you want to become. That's how you get there.

## Make Reviews Your Silent Marketing Team

Up to 90 percent of customers decide if they trust you before they ever talk to you. How? By reading your reviews. Before they click, call, or commit, they're scanning Google, Yelp, Instagram, YouTube, LinkedIn, and every line in between. That's why we treated reviews like revenue. We built automation into our CRM to request them after every service, we trained techs to personally ask for them, and we even gave spiffs to employees who earned the most five-star reviews. Reviews are digital referrals. The more you have, the more trust you win before you ever show up. Ask for them, respond to them, then repurpose them into ads, landing page quotes, and social proof across every touchpoint so that you control the narrative.

## Operationalize Your Superconsumer

From sales scripts to hiring questions, every function should be influenced by your superconsumer. Our ads and sales scripts spoke their language. Our techs were trained to serve them specifically. Our sales team practiced overcoming their unique objections. And our interview process weeded out anyone who wouldn't. When you hire, train, and sell with your best customer in mind, your entire business starts speaking their language, solving their problems, and exceeding their expectations.

## GO FROM SEEN TO CHOSEN

You can outspend the competition, or you can outsmart them.

Next up is the seven-letter word that made customers choose us—and never leave.

Chapter Summary

- Start small and stand out. Don't wait for the perfect budget or plan. Launch with memorable moves that make noise where your superconsumers are.
- Focus relentlessly on your superconsumer. Demographics tell you *where* to market; psychographics tell you *what* to say.
- Brand before you expand: Consistency is key.
- Measure CAC by channel so you can triple down on what works.
- Leverage drip campaigns to get customers to spend more up front, spend more often, and spend longer.
- Spend like the business you want to become.

SEVEN

PREMIUM





P est control license #8906.

That was Green Mango. That meant 8,905 pest
control providers came before us and thousands more would
follow. That's right: Nearly 9,000 competitors had opened
shop in a state with just seven million people.

How many pest control companies can you name? Three?
Four? Maybe five?

Exactly.

Most of them faded into irrelevance. They were squeezed
out of the market, sold for scraps, or folded entirely. I believe
that's because they did what everyone else did—compete on
price, pack in more stops per day, cut service times, dilute product, hire fast and train slow, and so on.

Pest control is often a race to the bottom that the big, established players almost always win because they have the deepest

pockets to leverage economies of scale. They lower their costs by operating at volume, enabling them to undercut smaller competitors without losing money.

As Patagonia's founder, Yvon Chouinard, warned, "If you want to be successful in business you don't go up against Coca-Cola or these big companies. They will kill you."

Instead, he said, you just do it differently.

Let's talk about how we did it differently and how you can, too.

From day one, the day we were assigned #8906, we knew Green Mango needed to stand out. Back then, every pest control company looked and felt the same.

Picture it: beat-up white pickup trucks desperately begging for a coat of fresh paint and a simple wash. Equipment spilling out of the truck bed like a sign of their carelessness. Tired techs dressed in casual clothes that, at best, had a faded company logo hidden somewhere, anywhere. Those same techs were armed with nothing more than hand cans and backpacks that didn't stand a chance against desert-dwelling pests like scorpions. It was like showing up to a gunfight with a squirt gun.

That was the norm.

If we were going to deliver on our promise to be the biggest and the absolute best, we couldn't be just another number in a sea of sameness. We needed a strategy that would rewrite the rules. Alex Hormozi has a rule for winning in business. If you open a sandwich shop, don't make a good sandwich. Make it so good that the second someone takes a bite, they stop and say, "Damn. This is the best sandwich I've ever had."

Tim Ferriss calls it the "one big domino." If you get this one thing right, the thing that truly separates you, everything else shrinks into irrelevance.

I call that one thing *premium*.

From day one, we decided to live (or die) by it. If I were into tattoos, I'd have *premium* inked across my forehead. That's how much it meant to me—and *us*.

From the moment a Green Mango truck pulled into your driveway, you could see the difference. Custom-painted flat-black with gleaming 22-inch rims, our trucks made our competitors' battered white ones look comical. Theirs were dented. Ours were flawless. We paid for proprietary paint jobs, daily washes, and biweekly repairs. (As our fleet grew, every truck was inspected weekly. The rule for our crew was: fail an inspection, sacrifice your bonus. That's how serious we were about being premium.)

When our technicians approached your door, the difference continued. They weren't allowed to wear whatever clothes they happened to throw on that morning. Instead, they wore professional, company-issued Nike uniforms from head to toe.

While every other tech from every other company preached spraying three feet up and three feet out like a broken record, our techs talked to customers about our one-of-a-kind Tri-Bloc technology. Forget three feet; we gave them three massive barriers of protection from pests. We sprayed the fence line, the yard, *and* the perimeter of the home. The result was better protection and no scorpions. Nobody else could promise that.

Our competitors packed 18 stops into each technician's daily route. We capped ours at 12. Other companies blasted homes with chemicals for five minutes. We spent at least 30 minutes meticulously treating each property. They used two to three gallons of product. We used at least 15. Their products carried risks. Ours were safe near pets, plants, and children.

My point is, from start to finish, we always chose the harder path—the premium path—but by year three and four, our commitment to premium was one of many reasons we were struggling financially.

After years of foregoing a salary, let alone a single draw, Dusty and I continued to pour every dollar right back into the business. And yet we could have easily multiplied our margins overnight simply by conforming to industry norms. At any moment, we could have flipped the switch, shown a healthy profit, and started paying ourselves. Of course it was tempting. On the flip side, though, by sacrificing *quality* for *quantity*, we also would have killed our customer base. It would have been a bait and switch. They wouldn't have continued to pay our premium prices for an average service.

Worse, we would've become just another number, indistinguishable from the 8,905 that came before us.

The pest control industry already had its Walmart, its TJ Maxx, its Old Navy: companies providing ordinary service at competitive prices. What it didn't have was its lululemon—a premium provider that customers would happily pay more for and brag about to their friends.

Lululemon founder Chip Wilson faced this same pressure while building his athletic apparel empire. While others sold $30 workout pants, he sold $100 ones by obsessing over his version of premium.

The product was better, but so was the experience. Every store had enough dressing rooms so no one waited. Hang tags were on the same side of every item so they were easy to find. Pricing and sizes on those tags appeared in bigger font sizes than most, so customers could spot them quickly and waste no time searching. Three-way mirrors eliminated the need for employee assistance. Every register was optimized to check you out in seconds.

Lululemon competed on quality, not price, and built a billion-dollar empire. Patagonia did the same. Chouinard built his empire by designing a better piton (the spike that is driven into a rock or crack to support a climber). Pitons evolved into building better crampons, then better ice axes, then better gear. Patagonia's very first mission statement was "Make the best product, period."

But what about Green Mango?

Nearly half a decade in, when the financial pressure was crushing us, we were forced to make a decision. Were we okay being Walmart, or TJ Maxx, or Old Navy? Should we become just another forgettable number? Just another pest control company scraping by on paper-thin margins?

*No. Heck no.*

We were #8906, and we would be different—even if it killed us.

So we maintained our premium standards when it hurt the most. We kept our service times long, our products top-notch, our applications thorough, our trucks immaculate, our techs on point, and our personal bank accounts *empty*.

I believe that decision ultimately defined our success and drove our valuation far beyond industry norms.

Two things can be true at once. It's why Dusty and I continued to be unable to pay ourselves for a few more years, but it's also why Green Mango was acquired for nearly nine figures while the other 8,905 Arizona-based pest control companies weren't.

Let's get into what I now call The Premium Effect, the counterintuitive business principle that transformed our business and could transform yours.

# THE PREMIUM EFFECT

In my experience, the third and fourth years of business are when most companies abandon their premium aspirations. With startup capital depleted and profitability still elusive, everyone faces the temptation to cut corners—reduce quality, lower prices, and in our case, pack in more stops.

It's a nasty roller coaster ride to the bottom that we refused to join. We refused to skimp on time or chemicals, like everyone else does. We decided to continue to be the exception to the rule. We continued delaying gratification. We were convinced it'd be worth it.

We played the long game, we continued to accept short-term pain for long-term gain, and we hoped for the best, knowing we were already experiencing the worst: no pay and lots of spray.

It did the trick.

By not packing routes, we had time to drive results up and reservices down. By using premium product, we could guarantee scorpion control. Because we maintained our trucks, they consistently attracted a flood of leads that we turned into up to

100 new accounts per month. Since we provided a premium experience, referrals multiplied.

By doing the exact opposite of what everybody else did, we got the opposite results: People bragged about their bug man, they told their friends, they shared on social media, and they stuck with us.

While most companies try to find "blue oceans" of uncontested market space, we won in a "red ocean" of fierce competition by creating our own category of *premium* pest control.

We weren't competing with 8,905 other pest control companies because none of them were doing what we did.

If we'd flipped the switch and skimped on quality, we would never have experienced the growth that we did. Backpack sprayers would have made us just another #8907 or #8908 —interchangeable and ultimately forgettable. We would have hit that seven-figure ceiling like everybody else.

Chouinard points to the Strategic Planning Institute's annual Profit Impact of Market Strategy (PIMS) report, which analyzes thousands of companies and repeatedly shows quality, not price, has the highest correlation with business success.

The numbers are mind-blowing. Companies with high product and service quality reputations average ROI rates 12 times higher than their low-quality, lower-priced competitors.

Think about your industry. How many competitors are you up against? There are more than 8,905 pest control businesses in Arizona, more than 19,800 authors on LinkedIn, and more than 90,000 gyms in the US.

In crowded markets where everyone competes on price, premium becomes your unfair advantage—the secret weapon that makes you stand out and delivers a proven 12× ROI.

It will take time and sacrifice, as it did with us, but I can promise you it pays off in more ways than one.

# HOW PREMIUM CHANGES EVERYTHING

Below are just a handful of tangible ways being premium helps you build to sell.

## Price Becomes Irrelevant

Nobody buys lululemon leggings because they're cheap. They buy them because they fit better, last longer, and feel premium. In the same way, nobody buys a Louis Vuitton bag for the stitching; they buy it for the status, the experience, the exclusivity.

Nobody chose Green Mango because we were the cheapest. We charged more than anyone else in the market, yet we thrived because we added value in ways our competitors wouldn't.

For example, delivering on our scorpion-free guarantee meant using specialized, premium products and spending at least 30 minutes at each stop instead of just five.

It cost us more, but it was worth it: Our ideal customers didn't flinch at our pricing because we were solving a problem nobody else could. They knew, as Warren Buffett said, "Price is what you pay. Value is what you get."

I applied this practice beyond pest control, too.

When selling Green Mango, instead of shopping for the cheapest attorney, I sought out the absolute best. I willingly paid an extra six figures for my lawyer because he made one promise no one else would. "My clients don't lose their rolled equity," he said. Every other attorney I spoke with, who all charged a fraction of what he did, told me, "Don't count on that money."

## Premium Customers Spend More Money

At Green Mango, customers initially signed up for general pest control (GPC), but many added multiple specialty services over time because they had the means and motivation to take us up on upsells and cross-sells that drove their LTV through the roof.

It's like Apple customers buying iPhones, then adding on charging docks, cables, AppleCare, and cloud storage before eventually expanding to MacBooks, iPads, and AirPods.

Premium pricing automatically filters out the price-sensitive tire-kickers, making room for the exact customers you want—those with both the means and willingness to invest in quality.

It's the difference between a budget hotel guest demanding refunds and a Four Seasons guest tipping the staff.

## Premium Customers Do the Selling for You

Johnjay, a legendary Phoenix radio host with a massive audience, had an ant problem. When his regular pest control provider offered the standard response—a days-long wait—Dusty rushed to Johnjay's home that same night.

That's premium.

The next morning, Johnjay spent 10 minutes on-air raving about Green Mango. We sold 20 new accounts that same day. Back then, we'd be lucky to sell 20 accounts with a team of 10 people knocking doors for an entire day. Then, because we delivered a premium customer experience, all of those new customers referred their friends, too.

Dusty clearing ants at a moment's notice became one of our first big breaks. It opened our eyes to other ways of growing, helped us eventually get off the doors for good and start scaling through media-driven marketing and advertising channels like radio, billboards, and more. Again, it was all because we were premium.

## Nobody Can Steal Your Customers

Competition is relentless in every industry, but in pest control, it's like war. Door-to-door sales reps will say anything to poach a customer, unless that door is answered by a Green Mango customer.

The truth is, they didn't even bother trying to convert our customers because they knew it was a lost cause. We heard it straight from the field: Competing reps stopped knocking on Green Mango customer's doors because they knew nobody would switch.

Imagine the competitive advantage of knowing your customer base is so loyal that others have given up trying to poach them.

By being premium, you can become untouchable.

## Premium Businesses Are Recession-Resistant

The COVID-19 pandemic crushed businesses around the world. Restaurants shut down, retail stores collapsed, and entire industries evaporated overnight.

Meanwhile, Green Mango just kept growing. People were home more than ever before, and when you're home all day, you notice things you normally wouldn't. If they had poor pest control, they saw the bugs. If they didn't have pest control, they wanted it. After all, Arizona is a desert—there's always something crawling around. With pest control suddenly top of mind, and the shortcomings of ordinary providers clearer than ever, everyone wanted the best protection possible. That led them to us.

Our experience proved that premium brands are more likely to survive, and even thrive, during downturns than brands competing on price. For example, Equinox survived the COVID-19 pandemic. 24-Hour Fitness filed for bankruptcy.

## Premium Means the Job Gets Done Right the First Time

Even though we offered free reservices (a premium feature), we rarely had to perform them. Our monthly reservice rate was below one percent—an unheard-of number in an industry where five to seven percent is the norm.

Research consistently shows that while only a small percentage of dissatisfied customers will complain about problems, up to 96 percent of customers who experience issues will disappear forever, taking their lifetime value with them.

When you do it right the first time, customers don't complain. They don't haggle. They don't demand refunds.

They buy more, they refer friends, and they make your business exponentially more profitable.

Who doesn't want that?

## Premium Multiplies Your Value

All these premium advantages meet at one critical point, the point that matters most when you're building to sell: business valuation.

Competitors built their business on thin margins, high churn, and endless callbacks. We built ours differently. It wasn't luck; it was premium execution at every level. It's why Green Mango wasn't valued like a typical pest control company. Instead, it was valued like a premium brand.

One acquisition offer letter spelled it out verbatim, citing our "reputation for quality" as a primary reason for our record-setting valuation. That's the premium effect in action—right there, written in black and white, next to a number that blew my mind.

Like I said, premium pays off. Every single time.

# FINDING WAYS TO BE PREMIUM

Now that you understand *why* premium pays off, let's talk about how to implement it. At Green Mango, we created premium experiences at every price point, from significant investments to completely free gestures that competitors overlooked.

You can, and should, do the same.

Our most visible investments in premium service were unmistakable: our truck-mounted power sprayers and Honda gas-powered pumps, which provided superior protection where competitors couldn't reach.

The two hats every tech had on hand at every home: the "door hat" for interacting with the customer, the "spray hat" for spraying the home. The Nike kicks: black, gray, or Green Mango green, always. The iPads that easily paid for themselves with upsells. The 22-inch rims, the extended truck cabs, the flawless paint jobs, and more.

Even our promotional merchandise reflected our premium standards. While most companies hand out standard, cardboard-like Gildan T-shirts, we invested in quality swag people wanted to wear. You'd see our merch at the gym, around town, creating walking billboards from people proud to represent our brand.

## Premium Does Not Have to Cost Anything

What's equally powerful, though, are the premium touches that cost nothing at all. It doesn't have to be crazy or extravagant. Little things make a big difference.

For example, we always reminded customers of their next service visit 48 hours in advance, then followed up again when their tech was on their way. Plus, *they* chose how we communicated with them—call or text. Inside the home, we always wore shoe covers. If we used their hose, we coiled it back neatly afterward. We made sure backyard gates were always closed and locked to prevent lost pets, wandering children, or, at homes with pools, something far worse.

If their shoes were scattered by the doormat, we'd organize them. We'd reposition the doormat itself if it was out of whack. We'd bring in garbage cans left out front. Our techs were trained to triple-check for spider webs while preparing the property, while spraying, and while dusting—in that order.

We'd knock on the door before and after every service; knowing we only see most clients every other month, we wanted to take advantage of every opportunity to build a relationship.

Of course, we're not the only ones to go above and beyond.

Four Seasons staff members greet you by name as you walk throughout the property: "Hello, Mr. Bawden." They make eye contact. They stop what they're doing when you approach with a question. "How can I help, Mr. Bawden?" They know why you're there: "Happy anniversary, Mr. Bawden." Rather than pointing you to the bathroom, they walk you to it. These little gestures cost nothing but create enormous value.

At Chick-fil-A, it's as simple as two words: "My pleasure." Those two words, delivered consistently with a smile, have helped the chain more than double McDonald's average sales per store, despite being closed on Sundays. I can't emphasize this enough: Those two words cost nothing.

What about you? What can you do for your customers? How can you start providing a premium service or experience today? If we can do it in pest control and they can do it in fast food, why can't you do it, too?

Hopefully, those examples got your creative juices flowing. Use them to start being premium now. As you can see, it will pay off.

## The Way You Do One Thing Is the Way You Do Everything

"Does Trainual make every manual look this nice?" she asked while scrolling through our digital training manuals.

My answer was simple. "No. We make every manual look that nice *before* we put it into Trainual."

Premium isn't something we just turned on when customers were watching; it was a standard that impacted everything we did. Our marketing team understood this, our technicians lived it, and our office staff embodied it.

When most companies talk about customer experience, they focus exclusively on customer-facing touchpoints. However, premium organizations understand that external excellence begins with internal excellence.

Our office reflected the same standards we delivered to customers: no trash on the ground, clean workspaces, organized supplies. Our trucks never left oil stains on customers' driveways—a small detail that others overlooked. Even our internal meetings followed premium protocols that included starting on time, following clear agendas, and ending with actionable takeaways.

I often use the example of a typical doctor's office to illustrate the exact opposite of premium. What happens when you visit a doctor? At the front desk, they rattle off a laundry list of questions. "What's your date of birth? Do you smoke? Drink? What medications are you taking? What have you taken in the past? Any allergies?"

Then you get led to your room, where the nurse asks those same questions *again*. And just when you think you're done, the doctor walks in and—you guessed it—starts from the top.

That's not premium. That's annoying.

We flipped the script by putting ourselves in the customer's shoes. If a homeowner had to re-explain their scorpion sightings, termite concerns, or mosquito bites to every Green Mango employee they met, we'd already failed.

Repetition kills trust, so instead of showing up with a clipboard and blank stare, our technicians knocked with purpose: "I'm here to take care of the scorpions you saw near the back patio, and I see a note about ants in the kitchen too. Is there anything else you'd like me to focus on today?"

That kind of service—where the customer doesn't have to start from scratch, where they feel seen, heard, and prioritized—isn't just professional; it's *premium*. It says: We remember, we're prepared, and we care enough to connect the dots so you don't have to.

That's why our sales team and technicians meticulously documented customer preferences in our CRM. We invested in training to ensure every technician knew to review those notes before every service call. Carol has a scorpion problem, Grace always wants a call 30 minutes before arrival so she can open the gate, Frankie would like the interior to be treated at every visit, Jim requests service for both garages—and every Green Mango tech knows it.

You see this principle everywhere once you start looking. Apple's immaculate packaging reflects the same attention to detail as their products. Even my podcast is called "The Premium Mindset" because premium isn't just what you do; it's how you think.

You can't deliver a premium experience through a mediocre organization. The way you do one thing truly is the way you do everything, and your customers can *sense* it, even if they can't always *see* it.

The premium approach that attracted our customers ultimately attracted our acquirers, delivering the same result: a willingness to pay more for something exceptional.

Even if it costs you nothing, it will be the best investment you ever make, because in a sea of sameness, premium is the surest way to stand out.

# PRO TIPS FOR BEING PREMIUM BY DESIGN

Here are a few more ways to build premium into your business, one intentional choice at a time.

## Make It Consumer-Facing

We branded our premium approach at Green Mango so that both customers and employees could instantly recognize what made us different. It was built into every script for sales and service. Every service visit began with, "I'll be performing your premium service today," followed by a detailed explanation of our proprietary Tri-Bloc technology.

By explicitly naming and explaining our premium elements, we achieved three things: Customers understood exactly what they were paying for, employees reinforced our premium positioning with every interaction, and we instantly elevated ourselves above the competition.

If you don't explicitly tell customers what makes you premium, they might never notice. Brand your difference, explain it consistently, and watch your value grow.

## Ask Grandma

I often relied on a simple internal question to guide our premium decisions: "What would you do for Grandma?" If you were servicing her home, how would you treat it? You can replace Grandma with any family member. The point is, thinking of Grandma became our North Star for discovering untapped opportunities to deliver premium experiences.

If Grandma was stuck on the side of the road, would you change a tire for her? One of our techs, Mark, pulled over in his Green Mango truck and put his training to use helping a total stranger fix a flat. I'd be shocked if she's not a Green Mango customer for life. Surely, people driving by saw that too.

That's not all. One afternoon, a tech named Dave arrived at a home that had three-foot weeds covering the side yard. Dave knew that our product only worked its best when it could reach the soil directly. That'd be impossible with so much overgrowth.

Without hesitation, he got down on his hands and knees and started pulling weeds. He didn't do it because it was in the manual or because anyone told him to. Knowing Dave, I'm sure he didn't even want a pat on the back. He did it because it was the right thing to do to deliver premium results.

Out of 44,000 Green Mango customers, that one homeowner went out of their way to contact me personally: "I want you to know you have an amazing technician." Even if we had somehow botched their next three, 13, or 30 services, I knew they'd remain loyal customers for life, all because Dave identified an opportunity to be premium by treating that customer's home like Grandma's.

## Incentivize Premium Behavior

Dave earned our "Above & Beyond" badge for the weed-pulling initiative I just mentioned.

Another tech, Kevin, earned his through profound human connection. Upon noticing a St. Jude's sign at a customer's home, he discovered the family had lost a child. Having experienced a similar loss himself, he spent 30 minutes simply listening and offering comfort. In those 30 minutes, a genuine bond was built.

When I heard about this interaction (which happened to involve someone connected to my family, though Kevin had no idea), I recognized something invaluable: That kind of authentic care can't be taught in training manuals.

Above & Beyond badges came with public recognition and financial bonuses. More importantly, we shared these stories in company meetings, creating a culture where premium behavior became the norm, not the exception. As I've said before, what gets rewarded gets repeated. Create a system that celebrates employees who go beyond expectations, and soon exceptional service becomes part of your businesses' DNA.

## Adopt the Premium Mindset Today

Chip Wilson was convinced his customers were *making* $100 every time they shopped at lululemon. Wilson recalled, "I knew that they were time-constrained. And if they could get in and out of a store in under 10 minutes with exactly what they wanted, then I was actually saving them $100 or $200."

That was his premium mindset.

Similarly, Yvon Chouinard saw himself as more of a craftsman than a businessman. While these mindsets aren't mutually exclusive (two things can be true at once), his premium mindset drove him to make decisions based on quality and integrity rather than short-term profit.

At Green Mango, we had "Premium" in our sales and services scripts, lighting up the wall behind me in neon green text during every "Premium Mindset" podcast recording, and even printed on our gear with sayings like "Premium or death."

The premium mindset means viewing every business decision through the lens of excellence rather than expedience, and like anything, it starts at the top with you.

## Create Generational Loyalty

Ever hear of a kid wanting to be a bug man for Halloween? We did, and when my team caught wind of it, they gave the little boy a premium bug man sticker and watched his face light up. Then they decked him out in Green Mango gear. A hat, a shirt, our sleeves, the works. We already had customers for life: his parents. Now we had customers for generations. (As a bonus, I didn't even know this was all happening. A tech told their manager, and the manager made it happen. That's proof that *everyone* took being premium to heart.)

Look at your business as it exists today. Would a buyer specifically cite your "reputation for quality" as a key value driver in an offer letter? If not, you're leaving millions on the table.

While license #8906 started as just another number in a sea of competitors, our commitment to premium transformed it into a winning ticket worth tens of millions. Now the question isn't whether you can afford to be premium; it's whether you can afford *not* to be.

Businesses don't die from being too premium. They die from being too forgettable. Which will you be?

## Chapter Summary

- In a crowded market, premium is the "one big domino"—the single strategy that can give your business an unfair advantage.

- Quality, not price, has the highest correlation with long-term business success.
- The way you do one thing is the way you do everything.
- Being premium doesn't have to cost you anything. Small touches can create massive impact.
- Premium customers pay more, refer more, and stay longer.
- Premium businesses command premium valuations.

# EIGHT

# PERFORMANCE

*"If you don't know where you are going, you'll end up someplace else."*
–Yogi Berra

In 2023, more than a year before I sold Green Mango, I did something that would have been unimaginable in our earlier days.

I left.

Forget a long weekend; I was gone for an entire month. My wife, kids, and I flew halfway around the world to Thailand, a place I'd never been, to do something I'd never done: unplug completely.

It wasn't just my first time leaving North America—it was my first time leaving the business behind without worrying about it collapsing. While employees worry about what'll pile up on PTO, we founders don't stress about what might pile up in a day. We stress the whole thing might fall apart in an hour.

At one point, I had three cell phones just to keep up with

everything. Even after I consolidated to one, my kids would beg to break my phone just to get their dad back.

In Thailand, I barely touched my phone. I took a few calls, responded to a few emails, and that was that.

For the first time, I wasn't splitting time between our first-born (the business) and my actual kids. Instead, I was fully present. What's more, I was able to fully disconnect from work and fully reconnect with the kids.

We zipped scooters down winding island roads too narrow for cars, wandered through ancient temples where golden Buddhas towered above us, and exchanged fist bumps with monkeys that studied us like we were the zoo animals.

My daughter stood wide-eyed, mesmerized by girls her same age with golden rings stacked around their necks, a cultural tradition so foreign and beautiful it froze her in place. My son struck a giant gong for good luck and hugged a real tiger like it was a stuffed animal.

When I approached, the same tiger accepting hugs from my seven-year-old turned its head and locked eyes with me like I was lunch. "If the tiger looks at you," its handler warned, "look away and get up slowly." Banks got a framed photo. I bailed before I became its next meal.

Another day, we hiked deep into the jungle with a family of elephants, fed them by hand, scrubbed mud from their backs, and cooled off in the river together. When rain came pouring down over the treetops, we stood there soaked, laughing like one big, muddy, happy family. It felt like something out of a movie. I swear the elephants were laughing too.

That's just a glimpse of what we experienced that month. Just like those flights with my dad when I was a kid, this trip changed me. Only now I was the one showing *my* kids the world.

It was the kind of experience my kids will tell their kids

about, the kind of memories I'll relive forever, and it was only possible thanks to the kind of freedom I never thought I'd have.

While I was 8,000 miles away fist-bumping monkeys, feeding elephants, and wearing just one hat—my Dad hat—Green Mango *thrived*.

That month, we hit 38 percent profit margins—in the middle of summer, when margins typically bottomed out. It was our most profitable month ever, and I was on another continent. Ten years earlier, I was spraying houses in Maricopa dreaming of a Saturday off. Now my business was printing millions more—without me knocking doors, spraying homes, fighting fires, or lifting a finger.

Of course, none of that happened overnight.

It took more detours than I can count. It took battle-tested systems. It took the right people in the right seats. It took sales and marketing working together as one. It took premium service our competitors couldn't match.

And it took KPIs.

Just a few years before that trip, I really only analyzed our numbers maybe once a year. Our goals were vague. Our plans were fuzzy. The business was growing, but we were leaving millions on the table without even knowing it. By the time I saw the numbers—and really looked at them—it was always too late to make meaningful changes.

When it came to the data, I was operating like an old-school baseball scout: mostly by feel.

As Billy Beane proved in *Moneyball*, feel only gets you so far. If you want to beat the big players, you need the right numbers. At Green Mango, we evolved from glancing at our numbers at the end of the year to leveraging them to drive the year.

That's the only reason I even felt comfortable leaving the state, let alone the continent. It was the very reason I could.

When I slipped away, nobody was shocked by our success. Not because they didn't like having me around (though I'm sure some enjoyed the break), but because the business was built to perform.

Everyone knew where we were going and exactly how we'd get there. As Yogi Berra said, "If you don't know where you're going, you'll end up someplace else."

Our key performance indicators (KPIs) are what propelled us to exactly where we wanted to go.

In the following pages, I'll show you exactly how we used them to create predictability, performance, and peace of mind.

My family and me in Thailand

# CLEAR KPIS DRIVE PREDICTABLE PERFORMANCE

We weren't surprised we broke records because we could already see it coming. That's the power of KPIs: Possible becomes probable, probable becomes predictable, and predictable becomes inevitable.

Buyers love that level of certainty. They want to know that if they put a nickel in, they'll get a quarter out. It's the same money math as marketing: If they can flood the machine with nickels and reliably pull quarters, they'll do it all day long. And with deeper pockets than most founders, they'll happily pay a fortune for a machine that operates like that.

Think of running your business without KPIs like driving cross-country without a map. Now imagine making that same cross-country trek with GPS guiding you every step of the way. Your goal is the destination. Your KPIs are the turn-by-turn directions. Every business and every department needs both: goals and KPIs, or direction and data. One tells you where you're going. The other shows you how to get there.

When our leadership team and I got as serious as Billy Beane about KPIs, we began *engineering* our future. Monthly projections became monthly realities. Annual targets became annual achievements. The seven-week rotation? The 38 percent profit margins? No fluke. The business was humming like never before.

It was all by design, because we weren't guessing anymore.

But let's be honest: Numbers make a lot of people's eyes glaze over. They feel overwhelming, intimidating, even cold.

That's why we treated KPIs like LEGOs. Every number was just a brick, and one brick at a time, we built the future we wanted. You can do the same for your business.

## THE LEGO FRAMEWORK

Give a kid a pile of LEGOs, and they'll build anything—a tower, a spaceship, even an entire city. Give an entrepreneur the right KPIs, and I believe they can do the same.

We adults see the picture on the LEGO box and think, *no way*. Then a seven-year-old sits down and starts snapping pieces together. Next thing you know a castle scrapes the ceiling, the Millennium Falcon looks just like the movies, or a whole empire rises from the floor.

The same child still mastering how to tie their shoes can build a 1,000-piece spacecraft from scratch because they're not building the Millennium Falcon; they're just connecting one piece at a time.

That's the genius of LEGO.

Business works the same way.

At Green Mango, we didn't walk in each day saying, "Let's become a $50 million business today." Instead, we focused on the bricks—our KPIs—that would get us there: average contract rate, LTV, CAC, and more.

Think of KPIs like LEGOs. Each one snaps into place,

stacking piece by piece toward something bigger. Together, those bricks predictably added millions to our top line (and bottom line). Even the biggest goals become achievable when you break them into smaller pieces you can actually build with.

The following is the LEGO Framework we used to make achieving massive goals feel as simple as stacking bricks.

## Step 1: Start With the Box

Just like any LEGO set, you start with the picture on the box—the goal. It shows you exactly what you're building.

Maybe you want to write a book this year, lose 25 pounds, hit $5 million in revenue, or finally shrink a nine-week service rotation down to seven. You approach it all the same way. Simply work backward using the LEGO Framework.

Rather than snapping random pieces together and hoping for the best, begin with the big picture, then reverse-engineer the bricks and pieces that bring it to life. The picture on the box is your goal. The bricks are your KPIs.

## Step 2: Begin With Your Biggest Bricks

Once you can see the picture on the box, dump out the pieces and grab the biggest ones. Big bricks are your core KPIs, the major metrics that move you forward.

No need to add numbers to them yet; just consider them categories that move the needle.

For example, books come from manuscripts. Manuscripts are made of words. Word count is your biggest brick for writing a book. For losing weight, your biggest brick, that core KPI, is pounds lost.

Think of this step like sorting through that pile of LEGO pieces—among hundreds of options, the pounds-lost brick stands out immediately. Just like the base plate of a castle or the main hull of the Millennium Falcon, it's the piece you build everything else around.

*BIG GOALS REQUIRE MORE KPIS JUST AS BIGGER LEGO SETS REQUIRE MORE PIECES*

A $5 million revenue goal requires multiple big bricks working together. Sales might track average contract rate, marketing might track CAC, operations might monitor route value or average service time, and customer service might focus on the save rate or retention.

Point is, each department needs at least one KPI.

You can think of each department's KPI(s) as the same brick in a different color.

When we shrank our nine-week rotation to seven, each department owned their piece: Routing owned efficiency metrics, technicians owned completion rate, and customer service owned rescheduling percentage.

If one team doesn't have a big brick, they're not connected to the build—and that puts your entire structure at risk.

## Step 3: Snap in the Small Bricks

Small bricks are time-based targets that make big bricks achievable.

Writing a book? Your big brick is a 60,000-word manuscript. That breaks down into these targets:

- 5,000 words per month (one chapter)
- 1,250 words per week (one-fourth of a chapter)
- 250 words per day (one page)

It's no wonder *New York Times* bestselling author Ryan Holiday says his secret to cranking out nearly a dozen bestsellers by his 35th birthday was as simple as writing "a couple crappy pages a day."

This is how the pros break down big goals.

Without small bricks, big bricks feel overwhelming. With them, even massive goals feel manageable.

## Step 4: Connect All Your Accessory Pieces

Not all pieces in a LEGO set are bricks. Some are weird little pegs, some are curved connectors, and some click into place behind the scenes.

They're completely different shapes that might not look like much, but without them the entire structure falls apart.

Accessory pieces are supporting KPIs and behaviors that help you hit your targets—different shape, same build.

A basketball player's free-throw percentage is a KPI, but his pre-shot routine—dribble three times, deep breath, set position—is a rhythm. Rhythms are the consistent behaviors that drive KPI results.

Put differently, KPIs are what you measure, and rhythms are what you repeat.

Every business needs both. At Green Mango, our customer service representatives had clear KPIs alongside critical rhythms: asking for referrals from every satisfied customer, smiling while talking on the phone, and greeting every visitor who entered our office.

Our service managers had essential rhythms like confirming all doors were locked, marking all stops on daily route sheets, and logging any writeups at the end of each day. When these rhythms became habits, KPIs automatically improved.

People perform better when they know what's coming next. It's why musicians warm up before concerts, it's why athletes stick to game-day routines, and it's why employees actually *appreciate* rhythms.

Anything that needs to be done consistently but can't be easily tracked numerically is a worthwhile rhythm. Find yours and make them non-negotiable.

For writing a book, accessory pieces might include:

- Writing first thing each morning
- Setting a 25-minute timer for focused work
- Outlining before drafting

For losing weight, accessory pieces might be:

- A 500-calorie daily deficit
- Thirty minutes of daily exercise
- Drinking 64 ounces of water a day

Now, let's take a look at how far we've come. For a $5 million revenue goal, big bricks might be:

- Average contract value (sales)
- CAC (marketing and sales)
- Reservice rate (customer service)

Small bricks break those down into time-based targets like:

- Monthly contract value
- Monthly CAC
- Monthly reservice rate

Then accessory pieces create supporting KPIs and behaviors like:

- Close rate
- Qualified leads per month
- Routine inventory inspections

Or take a service goal like shrinking your rotation from nine weeks to seven. Say our big bricks were:

- Completion rate (operations)
- Route score (routing)
- Average service time (technician)

Small bricks break those down into time-based targets like:

- Monthly completion rate
- Stops per week
- Average service time per stop

Then accessory pieces create supporting KPIs and behaviors like:

- Daily route sheet reviews
- Morning team huddles
- Heads-up/pre-arrival texts

This framework makes the impossible inevitable because one piece at a time, you build exactly what's pictured on the box.

## Step 5: Add the Extra Pieces

Every LEGO set comes with a few extra pieces. You know, just in case. Your KPI system should too.

For authors, it might be scheduling buffer days in advance, knowing life will get in the way around holidays.

For weight loss, it could be having equipment handy at home for days the gym is closed.

For businesses, it's the additional resources (floaters, techs, extra trucks) you'll need to hit your targets when unexpected challenges arise.

Plan for the unexpected. Build in margin.

## Step 6: Connect It All

Even with the right box, bricks, and pieces, there's one more step: connecting everything through incentives, training, and shared goals that motivate everyone to hit their targets and KPIs.

If one department's building a Millennium Falcon and another's building Hogwarts, you're not getting either.

You can't shorten a nine-week rotation to seven without alignment. When we tackled this at Green Mango, routing had to optimize density, techs had to complete routes on time, CSRs had to reduce reschedules, and service leads had to monitor reservice trends.

If any team failed, we all failed. But when everyone succeeded, we unlocked millions in additional revenue while providing better service.

## Building Your Own Masterpiece

Here's how to start putting this into play:

- Set a goal and bust out your org chart.
- Assign each department at least one core KPI.
- Break each core KPI into smaller, time-based targets.
- Add supporting KPIs and rhythms to hit targets.
- Add any resources needed to make the above feasible.

Then, like a seven-year-old sitting in front of a pile of LEGOs, get to work snapping pieces together and watch the impossible come to life.

# WHAT YOU SEE IS WHAT YOU GET

For years, I hoarded Green Mango's numbers like state secrets. I was afraid employees would calculate my salary, compare paychecks, or worse—see the business struggling during tough months.

You can't expect your team to hit a target they never see.

Think about what happens when your bank balance is out of sight. Spending increases, saving decreases. The same happens with your business metrics. Out of sight, out of mind.

A1 Garage Door Service has more than 65 locations across 14 states. Green Mango had two locations in one state.

Yet Tommy's entire A1 team knew their numbers, while mine flew blind. Tommy Mello, founder and CEO of A1 Garage Door Service, is the standard-bearer of the service industry. He catapulted his garage door business into a multi-million dollar juggernaut within a few short years.

"If your team doesn't know the numbers," he said to me, "how can they help you improve them?"

It's like asking them to win the game without showing them the scoreboard.

There's a fantastic parable that drives this home. A traveler asks three bricklayers what they're doing. The first mutters, "Laying bricks."

The second says, "Building a wall."

The third stands tall and declares, "I'm building a cathedral."

Same work, different vision.

If you want cathedral builders—and trust me, you do—they need to see the whole blueprint. That's why we made visible what was once invisible.

In our office, we printed every KPI on wall-sized canvases. CSRs saw their conversion rates daily in the bullpen. Technicians got a weekly scorecard texted straight to their phones, ranking them against their peers on KPIs like completion rate, call-outs, reservices, and sales. Marketing KPIs commanded attention in their workspace. Company-wide goals hung in the common area.

On top of that, every first Tuesday of the month, the whole team gathered. I flipped pancakes while each department head shared one simple metric: goal versus actual for every KPI.

We didn't just share numbers; we cast vision. We showed everyone exactly how their bricks were constructing our cathedral.

Just like that, we didn't have employees anymore; we had cathedral builders. People who caught problems early, proposed solutions, and collaborated without being asked.

We discussed our progress and our performance during every monthly meeting. Tommy calls his company-wide meetings "bringing the fire." At Green Mango, we brought the fire.

KPIS ARE YOUR GOLDEN TICKET

Those KPIs on our walls—the ones we shared every month over pancakes, the ones that guided every department, the ones that transformed bricks into a cathedral—they're like a passport to freedom.

Your Thailand might be different. Maybe it's coaching your kid's baseball team without checking emails between innings, maybe it's that RV trip you've been postponing for years, maybe it's finally writing that novel, learning to surf, or just being fully present at dinner.

Whatever it is, KPIs are how you get there. Those numbers make your business predictable. And predictability is what buyers pay premiums for, what lets you sleep at night, and what finally frees you from being the only one who can keep the lights on.

Start small. Pick one goal. Break it into bricks. Make them visible. Then watch as the impossible becomes inevitable, one measurable piece at a time.

Whatever your version of Thailand looks like, KPIs are your ticket there. Punch it.

# LAY THE FIRST BRICK TODAY

I implemented these principles at Green Mango far too late in my journey. Had I understood the power of properly structured KPIs from day one, we would have hit our goals faster and walked away with an even bigger payday.

KPIs aren't sexy. They're just numbers on a wall.

But what if those numbers are the difference between being stuck at your desk forever and being free to live your life? Between hoping your business works and knowing it will? Between dreaming about your exit and actually achieving it?

They are.

So don't wait. Pick one department. One KPI. One brick. Lay it now—and start building your business in a way that sets you free.

## Chapter Summary

- Goals show your team where they're going. KPIs

show them how to get there. Every department needs both.

- Think of goals and KPIs like LEGOs:
  - The box = your goal
  - Big bricks = core KPIs
  - Small bricks = time-based targets that support core KPIs
  - Accessory pieces = supporting behaviors and rhythms
- Everything must connect: KPIs only work when they're aligned across teams.
- Transparency drives ownership. Share progress regularly—in meetings, on walls, in scorecards—so every employee sees where they stand and how they contribute.

NINE

## FRIENDS AND MENTORS

*"One is too small a number to achieve greatness."*
–John C. Maxwell

My first mentor predicted my future while I was vandalizing a Christmas display.

My dad had brought me along to his friend Mark's house that evening. I was the quiet kid, about 12 years old, blending into the background while the adults stood around shooting the breeze.

Then Mark glanced across the street, pointed at his neighbor's house, and shook his head. "Still got the Christmas lights up," he said.

Those blazing lights were locally famous, drawing visitors from neighboring towns all season long. But at that point, it was March: We were far closer to spring break than Christmas. The season was over, and Mark's patience was wearing thin. The spectacle was doing nothing more than keeping him and his wife up at night as light bled through their bedroom blinds.

"I oughta rip those things down myself," Mark said. He was half-joking, but I was dead serious.

Without a word—without even thinking—I slipped away from the adults, tiptoed into the neighbor's yard, and launched into action. I darted from tree to tree like the Grinch, yanking down every light I could reach with an ear-to-ear grin plastered across my face.

Ten minutes later, the yard was dark as night. Problem solved.

When I returned to the garage, out of breath and buzzing with pure excitement, Mark looked down at me, then turned to my dad with a smirk. "Cameron's either gonna end up in jail or a millionaire, Clyde."

He wasn't wrong.

I now understand what Mark saw that night: wild initiative, zero hesitation, complete disregard for permission, and full commitment to finishing something nobody asked me to start. Many of those same traits have helped me as an entrepreneur, but they could've just as easily landed me behind bars.

I've known plenty of people who are wired like me who went both ways. Some built businesses, others built rap sheets.

Often, the difference was less about who they were *themselves* and more about who they were *around*. After all, instead of choosing their own path, most people follow the pack. Or as the Bible says, "He who walketh with wise men shall be wise: but a companion of fools shall be destroyed."

That's why I love the saying "Show me your friends and I'll show you your future."

We've always known the people around us influence us, but that line hits different when you see the research.

## YOU CATCH WHAT YOU'RE AROUND

In one of the largest studies ever conducted on human behavior, researchers tracked more than 12,000 people for 32 years and uncovered something wild: If just *one* of your close friends becomes obese, your chances of becoming obese skyrocket by 57 percent.

That means your chances of becoming obese could have less to do with your genetics or willpower and more to do with the CSR or sales rep you exchange a quick "hello" with at the office every morning.

Even crazier, *if a friend of a friend* becomes obese (someone you've never even met), your risk of packing on pounds to the point of obesity could increase by approximately 20 percent.

As organizational psychologist Dr. David Burkus puts it, "Your friends make you fat, but so do their friends, and so do their friends of friends."

Worse, it doesn't stop with weight.

If your friends smoke, you could be 61 percent more likely to light up. If your friend gets divorced, your chances of getting divorced shoot up 75 percent. Research even suggests that your income tends to rise or fall to match your peer group. That one proves the old adage true: Your *network* really is your *net worth*.

Like yawning, accents, or the flu, you catch what you're around.

That said, the most powerful evidence comes from workplace research by Dylan Minor and Michael Housman from the Kellogg School of Management: If you sit within 25 feet of a high performer, your own performance improves by 15 percent. But sit near a low performer, and your performance can sink by up to 30 percent.

In other words, this spillover effect suggests negative influences can be twice as contagious as positive ones.

Think of it like this: If you're closing $10,000 in monthly sales, sitting near a low performer could cut $3,000 a month just like that. Over a year, that's a plunge from $120,000 to $84,000 in total sales—a $36,000 loss just from desk placement.

This explains what Mark saw in that driveway years ago. My personality wasn't the only factor determining my future; my circle would either amplify my best traits or my worst. Business or jail wasn't just about me. It was about who surrounded me.

The good news is that this "social contagion" phenomenon can be your secret weapon. A cheat code for success. Think business, not jail.

As Dr. Mark Hyman explains, meaningful relationships lower stress, boost oxytocin, and even activate genes that protect against disease. The acclaimed physician goes so far as to compare relationships to "prescription-strength medicine for your mind, body, and soul."

That 15 percent improvement in performance means just sitting near a top performer could boost your monthly sales from $10,000 to $11,500—an additional $18,000 annually. For golfers, it's like improving your handicap from 15 to 12.8 just by choosing the right playing partners.

Think back to high school. Who were you closest with? Who did you run with? Who did *they* run with? Now think about where some of those people are today.

Did they grow into the kind of person you want to be around, or the kind you're glad you drifted away from?

The difference wasn't just *personality*. It was *proximity*.

I saw this power of proximity play out firsthand at a shooting range in the middle of nowhere.

My buddy Jamie was preparing to launch a business focused on active shooter training and executive retreats. He invited my friends and me to "Little Grand Canyon" for a test run, so he could work out the kinks before going live.

We were handling everything from ARs to pistols when Jamie suggested a competitive shooting drill. Two shooters stood side by side, each assigned a color—red or green. Targets popped up in unpredictable bursts, flashing the colors. Think Whac-A-Mole with guns and lights. With a limited number of rounds, the goal was simple: Mow down your color.

It was green versus red. Whoever hit the most of their assigned targets won.

"All right, Cam, you're up," Jamie called out. "You're green."

I went head-to-head with another novice like me in my first round, and we both fumbled through it, scoring six or seven points each. Not terrible for beginners, but nothing impressive either. The scores were as average as our skills.

Then Jamie stepped up beside me.

"Let's go, Cam," he said, nodding toward the targets. "Round two."

*Man, I got nothing to lose here,* I thought. Meanwhile, Jamie had everything to lose. He's a literal pro.

As I shouldered the pistol, I was suddenly hyperaware of Jamie's stance beside me, his breathing, his posture, all of it. I copied him. Why not? Then the buzzer went off. I fired, tracked, adjusted—locked in with a level of focus I didn't even know I had minutes earlier.

Final score: Jamie 18, me 14.

I stared at the scoreboard in disbelief. I'd doubled my performance without a single extra rep. No coaching, no extra practice rounds, no walkthrough. Just proximity.

The only thing that changed was who stood beside me.

Jamie noticed it too. I had shown up differently that round, just by shooting alongside him.

You see, when you're next to someone operating at a higher level, your brain automatically calibrates to their standard. You absorb their intensity, you mirror their movements, you start to think like they think. It's monkey see, monkey do for grownups.

Athletes experience this every day in practice. Entrepreneurs feel it in masterminds. Parents observe it in their kids.

"Iron sharpens iron."

During a break in the action, I had another realization. I looked around at the group I had assembled—14 guys, not one earning under $1 million a year. That wasn't a coincidence either.

The shooting range made visible what happens invisibly every day: We rise or fall to the level of those around us. There is no neutral influence.

Your circle isn't just a reflection of who you are now; it's a preview of who you'll become. Look around you. Look at your crew. Take it all in.

Do they give you the right motivation? Inspiration? Feelings? Do they push you to be a better version of yourself?

You're always catching what others do, so what are you catching? What's it gonna be? Jail or sale?

There's no question that proximity helps you rise or fall to the level of the room, but *belief* invites you into rooms you never knew existed. And nothing rewires belief faster than seeing someone do what you thought couldn't be done, because the right friends and mentors are capable of blowing the ceiling off what you thought was possible.

Like what happened to Dusty before we started Green Mango.

Me shooting

# SEEING IS BELIEVING

Before Green Mango, Dusty was selling pest control for another company.

He thought he was the man, and based on his performance, so did everyone else. He was closing three to six new accounts a day, which was easily pacing the office.

Then one Monday, he knocked on a door that knocked him back down to earth.

Around 10 am, Mike swung open his front door wearing a half-smile, half-smirk, as if he already knew something Dusty didn't.

He let Dusty pitch, listened politely, then asked, "You open to some feedback?"

Turns out, Mike had sold pest control for years. He even owned an entire branch in another state. In other words, he was the real deal.

Mike offered a few pointers, but what really stood out to Dusty was a number. "The top national reps," Mike explained, "they're selling 10 accounts a day."

*Ten? A day?*

Dusty's head was spinning as he walked away from Mike's home. What he had believed to be elite—three to six accounts a day—suddenly felt average. His entire belief blew up in a 10-minute conversation.

From that moment forward, 10 a day was Dusty's new standard. A man on a mission, he closed 10 new accounts that same day.

That's the story we shared with every new sales rep at Green Mango. It was baked into our sales manual and our DNA. As it turns out, achieving elite status has as much to do with belief as it does sales targets.

On that ordinary Monday, Mike—an unexpected mentor—shattered a ceiling Dusty didn't even know existed. He forever altered what Dusty believed could be done.

And as Mark taught me, we always do what we believe.

I call these pivotal encounters "watershed moments"—when someone else's example demolishes our own self-limiting beliefs. I've learned these moments almost always come from the friends and mentors in our lives.

You've experienced plenty of watershed moments yourself: the first time someone with your background bought a house you thought you couldn't afford, watching a friend quit a job they hated and start a business that took off, seeing a guy your same size throw down a dunk or bench 225 pounds like it's nothing.

These encounters permanently alter your sense of what's possible. Once you *see* what's possible, you start to believe it. And once you believe it, you can *achieve* it.

For example, what happened after Edmund Hillary and Tenzing Norgay summited Mount Everest in 1953 and lived to tell about it? More than 7,200 people followed—including a 13-year-old, an 80-year-old, and a man with no legs.

Hillary and Norgay's success transformed the impossible feat, an unclimbable mountain, from a death sentence that had already taken lives to an adventure to check off the ol' bucket list.

The mountain didn't change, but the belief sure did.

Rob was my Mike.

Rob wasn't loud or attention-seeking or braggadocious. He wasn't the kind of guy who'd walk into a room and command everyone's attention. In that way, he was like...me.

However, he was a millionaire, and when we crossed paths in the early days of Green Mango, a million bucks felt like a pipe dream to me.

The first time I met Rob, his wife rolled up in a clean white Escalade. A petite woman stepped out with a diamond on her finger that could have paid off my car. And there was Rob, just a regular guy running a restoration business, an industry no more glamorous than pest control.

That single encounter rewired something in my thinking: If he can do it in restoration, why can't I do it in pest control? More importantly, if he—someone like me—can make even just $1 million, why can't I? Why can't I be a millionaire, too?

Rob showed me what was possible, and from that point forward, I paid attention. I asked questions. I watched how he moved, and I modeled what worked.

Not long after, I achieved what previously seemed impossible: I made my first million.

That begs this question: If a man with no legs can summit the world's tallest mountain, why can't you?

The answer is that you can. You can achieve far more than you currently believe. You always could. But you won't believe it until the right person shows you what's possible.

That's the true power of friends and mentors. They show you what's possible. Seeing what's possible rewires your beliefs and elevates your thinking. And we do what we believe. So surround yourself with people who raise your standards, people who make you ask: *Why not me?*

# FRIENDS AND MENTORS ARE LIKE TOOLS

Fast-forward to today, and I think of friends and mentors the same way I think of tools.

At Green Mango, we use Slack for team chat, Field Routes for scheduling, and Trainual for onboarding and documentation. Each tool serves a specific purpose.

Would you use Slack to run payroll? Of course not. That'd be like trying to dig a tunnel with a teaspoon. Instead, you'd use the right tool for the right job.

That's why I believe in finding a mentor for each hat you wear. There's no one-size-fits-all when it comes to mentorship. I don't want one person guiding every area of my life; I want the right person helping me wear each hat better.

For instance, Tommy Mello systematizes his personal life like his business. His house cleaners follow checklists, and he's even floated the idea of offering them bonuses tied to spot-checked tasks.

The same mindset inspired me to systematize every aspect of Green Mango, then Tommy helped me explode our EBITDA and prepare for a premium acquisition. (As I mentioned earlier, the guy scaled A1 Garage Door Service to $200 million+, but he's also bought and sold more businesses than most people will ever work for.)

Mark Fournier helped me find peace when my finances were a 10 but my fulfillment was a 1. He introduced me to the life balance wheel and helped me expand my scores in all the right areas.

Casey Baugh gave me a preview of life after the exit. Between his Sandlot Partners portfolio and deep work around identity, legacy, and intentional living, he's helped me with life on the other side of Green Mango's acquisition.

Each of these guys filled a specific gap. None of them tried to do it all, and that's the point. Your goal is to find people who are strong where you are weak, period.

I'm not Mark Fournier. If you want to dive into the stuff that doesn't show up on a P&L but shows up in your marriage, your parenting, your presence, and your peace of mind, then Mark's your guy.

But if you're a service business owner trying to break through your ceiling and build to sell, I can help because I've been in your shoes—and because I don't pretend to be all things to all people.

Of the seven businesses I built, I consider two to be massive successes. As you know, Green Mango hit $27 million in annual revenue by the time I exited. Coconut Cleaning could end up doing more. Until then, I help business owners who are trying to reach that same level because I've actually been there.

This approach has become central to how I mentor others in my 1% Club. When a pool company owner comes to me on the verge of bankruptcy, I can advise because I navigated those exact waters. When a first-time founder struggles with scaling, I know the pitfalls because I've fallen into them.

## Make Sure Your Friends and Mentors Have Walked the Path You Want to Walk

Put differently, if you wouldn't trade *places* with them, don't trade *wisdom* with them.

You wouldn't ask your broke uncle how to build wealth or your single friend how to save your marriage, so don't try to learn from someone who hasn't lived it.

The right mentor has already climbed your Everest. They know where the air gets thin, where the ice gets slippery, or where the shortcuts look appealing but lead to nowhere. They'll guide you up the fastest route and keep you from tumbling down the mountain.

I like to find the right mentor for every hat I wear.

Once you've identified the right mentor, the next move is getting on their radar and eventually in the same room, so you can cultivate the relationship you want.

Let me show you how I've made that happen.

# MY "OUTSIDER TO INSIDER" APPROACH

How do you get in the room of those people who are bigger, better, and further down the road than you? Here's how I broke into Tommy, Casey, and others' inner circles—and how you can, too.

## Step 1: Find Common Ground

Just like in sales, build rapport first. Start with research, then ask relevant questions.

Ideally, ask them questions that tee up shared interests or topics they love that you uncovered through your research. Asking Tommy about shop tours was a winner because I knew he loves them.

Then connect on things outside of entrepreneurship too. When I learned Tommy was into golf and fitness, I made sure to ask about those areas rather than always talking shop.

These personal connections can create stronger bonds than any business discussion could. The key is finding genuine overlap where your interests and theirs naturally intersect.

## Step 2: Be Strategic About Access

Spend time where your ideal mentor would. That might be a certain gym, an airport lounge, a shooting range, an event, a mastermind group, you name it.

Remember the law of six degrees of separation: You're only ever six people away from your dream connection. Talk about who you want to meet. You never know who in your network already has that connection you're dreaming of.

When you secure that first meeting, bring a hype man—someone who can introduce your success instead of you having to do it yourself, because any sign of ego will burn bridges like nothing else.

Then, before the meeting ends, lock in a second encounter. Make it frictionless. Offer to cook for their team lunch. Schedule a tee time. Volunteer behind the scenes at their next event. Ask if you can feature them in a podcast episode. Make it so easy and valuable that saying "yes" is a no-brainer.

## Step 3: Stay Top of Mind

Be in the room even when you're not in the room.

I made it a point to interact with Tommy on social media, commenting on his posts and sharing his content. Plus, I made sure to acknowledge his personal milestones, like messaging him on his birthday or congratulating him on company achievements.

These things allowed me to stay on his radar.

That's a good start, but when the time's right, go even further to be in the actual room. I paid my own way to attend one of his live Freedom events in Florida, across the country, just to be there and show my support.

Do you think my presence went unnoticed? Of course not.

I know for a fact Tommy appreciated the effort because he told me so.

## Step 4: Give So Much It Hurts

What if your mentor was your most valuable customer—how would you serve them? How would you give value?

At Green Mango, we charged $10,000 to put any business's promotional materials in our new customer welcome packs. In other words, $10,000 to get in front of our more than 40,000 customers.

We put Tommy's business, A1 Garage Door Service, in there for free. I absorbed the $10,000 to make it happen. That's what I mean when I say give so much it hurts.

What can you give? How can you give even more? And more?

Be a giver, not a taker.

## Step 5: Be Someone They'd Want to Mentor

If you want to work with elite mentors, become the kind of person they'd want to mentor. That means the kind of person who asks great questions, builds real relationships, supports in more ways than one, and gives heaps of value.

# KEEP LEVELING UP

The people who got you here are not always the people who can take you there. The people who helped you start might not be the same ones who help you scale. Would you expect your middle-school basketball coach to guide you to the pros?

As your business evolves, your employees must evolve, as should your friends and mentors. Some people are built for the starting line—not the summit.

The opposite is also true: *You* have to be ready for the right mentor. If you're at level three, the person at level nine might be too far ahead to help you bridge the gap. Instead, you might be better suited connecting with the person at level four or five.

For example, when I was 12 years old, Mark Fournier was already in my life. Can you imagine Mark mentoring 12-year-old me?

That version of me couldn't have handled his wisdom. It would have gone in one ear and out the other. But when I was 25—successful on paper, struggling in real life—he was the perfect guy for the job.

Same with Casey Baugh. He wouldn't have made sense when I was in the trenches building Green Mango, but after I took my chips off the table, Casey helped me reimagine what life after business could look like. Same with Rob, and Tommy, and so on.

That's why I'm always checking for alignment: Is this person still the right one for the level I'm on—or the level I want to reach?

If your circle stays the same as your vision expands, you'll stall. Or worse, you'll shrink to fit. So what should you do?

If you're at $100,000 in revenue, don't chase someone at $15 million. The gap's too wide; the leap's too big. It'd be like a middle-school basketball player trying to get coached up by Steph Curry. But someone at $1 million? They just closed the gap you're standing in. It's like that same middle schooler getting coached up by a high schooler. They remember exactly what it takes and can get you there.

Then when you hit $1 million, you level up again. And again. That's how you keep climbing: step by step. Mentor by mentor. Room by room.

# THE IMPLEMENTATION EDGE

I can't emphasize this enough: The number one reason why people are successful is because they implement what they learn.

That's why Derek Sivers says, "If more information were the answer, we'd all be billionaires with six-pack abs."

The answer is *implementation*, not *information*.

Tommy illustrates this to a T. During shop tours of other businesses, while everyone else is nodding along, Tommy is furiously taking notes and firing off texts to his team to implement what he's learning in real time. It doesn't matter if we're visiting a $500,000 business or a $50 million operation—if Tommy spots something valuable, I can almost guarantee it's being implemented at A1 Garage Door Service before dinner. That's why he's built a $200 million company while others are still just collecting notes.

Don't be the person who just listens and takes notes but then never acts on them. If you haven't taken action, take a moment to reflect. What's stopping you? What's holding you back from implementing the changes or routines you know will make a difference?

Success isn't about what you learn—it's about what you implement.

# YOUR NETWORK IS YOUR NET WORTH

This principle has been shaping my life since I was a kid tearing down Christmas lights, and it continues to shape my success today.

I've come a long way from that night in Mark's driveway. The wild kid yanking down decorations has built businesses, made millions, and mentored others along the way.

But the fundamental truth remains the same: Your circle is your compass.

As Jim Rohn famously said, "You are the average of the five people you spend the most time with."

Choose wisely. Your future depends on it.

## Chapter Summary

- Your future depends on who you're around.
  Research shows your inner circle shapes everything from income and health to habits and happiness.

- Negative influences can be twice as influential as positive ones.
- Seeing is believing: The right friends and mentors shatter your self-limiting beliefs.
- Friends and mentors are like tools—there's no one-size-fits-all. Work with the right person to solve the right problem.
- Learn from people who've already walked the path you want to walk. If you wouldn't trade places with them, don't trade wisdom with them.
- Use my "Outsider to Insider" approach to level up your inner circle:
  - Find common ground.
  - Be strategic about access.
  - Stay top of mind.
  - Give so much it hurts.
  - Be someone they'd want to mentor.
- Keep upgrading your circle as you grow. The relationships that got you here may not get you there.
- Implementation always beats information.

TEN

EXIT

*"By failing to prepare, you are preparing to fail."*
–Benjamin Franklin

"Cameron, are you comfortable?" one of the voices asked.

Silence stretched across the call like static. A dozen buyers, brokers, and attorneys—most of them strangers—anxiously waited on my final word.

I took one last deep breath. Then, through the lump in my throat, I forced out a weak joke to lighten the mood. "No, I want to cancel. I changed my mind."

"Too late," Jane, the buyer's rep, fired back flat as paper.

And just like that...it was over.

I'd always pictured a boardroom with sweeping views. Champagne. Expensive pens. At the very least, a few firm handshakes.

Instead, I closed the biggest deal of my life on an ordinary Wednesday morning from a Chick-fil-A parking lot.

Just me, alone in my truck, watching the drive-thru line

inch forward as my life changed forever—my breakfast burrito growing cold beside me.

No champagne. No expensive pens. Not even a handshake.

The moment was so ordinary it felt surreal. I hung up, stared out the window, and broke down.

My phone buzzed seconds later. "How do you feel, Cam?" Dad asked.

"Kinda sad," was all I could manage.

I texted Lyss, "It's done." She rushed out of Ivory's cheer practice to call me. At that point I was bawling. She could barely make out a word between tears.

Fourteen years of blood, sweat, and sacrifice, signed away in a conference call shorter than most lunch breaks. It really was over.

I never thought the moment would feel so anticlimactic.

I guess that's because the real fireworks had already exploded in the grueling lead-up to that final closing call. The tears rolling down my cheeks weren't just about saying goodbye to Green Mango (which was harder than I ever imagined); they were a release. They were a purge of everything that came before: the relentless pressure, the 2 am strategy sessions, the daily interrogations, and all the last-minute legwork to close the deal that pushed my leadership team, my family, and me to the brink over six brutal months after signing the letter of intent (LOI) to close.

In most deals, due diligence makes up the bulk of the selling process. It's when buyers roll up their sleeves, comb through every part of your business (financials, contracts, systems, tax returns, customer data, HR, even your lease) and look for reasons to walk away or renegotiate. Sixty to 120 days is normal for due diligence, though in our case, due diligence lasted several months because we were not nearly as prepared as I hope you now will be.

Because of that, selling the business was every bit as hard as the first five years of building it combined.

Our diligence period included a never-ending quality of earnings (QoE) review that felt like a financial colonoscopy, as well as trademark battles, competitors trying to poach our people, north of $500,000 in lawyer fees, and our punk landlords demanding a cut just to swap a name on our office lease.

Put it this way: Our family vacation to Lake Powell in September 2024 was no Thailand. I spent that trip crouched in a closet on a houseboat, whispering into my phone during hours-long diligence calls while my daughter pounded on the door, her voice cracking as she begged me to come play.

That's the part nobody warns you about. You work just as hard to sell the business as you did to build it in the first place, especially if you didn't build to sell early on. I didn't. Green Mango grew into what I thought would be a legacy business. But then my kids started growing up before my eyes, I felt increasingly in over my head, and the offers pouring in became too good to ignore.

Here's what I've learned since that morning at Chick-fil-A: It doesn't have to be that way. The sales process doesn't have to be so incredibly intense...and long...and frustrating...and expensive. That's why I'm sharing with you what I know now. The brutal stress, the frantic scrambling, the sleepless nights, the ridiculous fees. Much of it can be avoided with the right preparation.

Selling your business is a lot like selling your house: the best time to prep is long before you list.

You don't repaint walls while buyers are walking through, just as you don't fix the plumbing during the open house. You make those improvements ahead of time, so that you appeal to buyers, create competition, and command top dollar. Better yet, every improvement, every upgrade, and every repair lets you live better in the meantime.

It's the same in business. That's the true power of building to sell.

Whether you plan to exit in three years or 30, building like you *could* sell tomorrow is the best thing you can do for your business *today*.

Allow me to save you the stress, the scramble, and the sleepless nights with the chapter I wish I'd read years before I said goodbye.

# THE THREE PILLARS OF A PREMIUM EXIT

Here's how most founders assume a sale goes:

Step 1: Go to market. Talk to buyers, then choose one to move forward with by signing an LOI.

Step 2: Due diligence. After the LOI is signed, that buyer digs deep. This includes a third-party QoE report to verify and validate every dollar you've claimed. (Like me, most founders underestimate the rigor here.)

Step 3: Close. If everything checks out, you finalize the deal. (Then hit refresh on your bank account all day, anxiously waiting for the money to appear and for it all to finally feel real.)

Now here's the thing most founders miss: Going to market isn't the first step; preparing to go to market is.

As one of my favorite sayings goes, "By failing to prepare, you are preparing to fail." That's why up to 80 percent of businesses that go to market never actually sell. And even the ones that do often go for pennies on the dollar, or founders leave millions on the table like I did simply because they weren't fully prepared.

They walk into diligence with too many unknowns and end up paying a multiple on *their* mistakes. For example, you pay a multiple on stress that spreads across the team. Taking diligence calls from a closet during my vacation was nothing compared to what James, our CFO, went through during those six months. You also pay a multiple on risk by giving the buyer more time and more reasons to renegotiate the deal based on what's uncovered, fixing everything that's incomplete, inaccurate, or just plain disorganized.

And then you might even pay a multiple on QoE, your third-party audit.

In our case, that third party was Deloitte, one of the Big Four accounting firms. We weren't just paying their premium rates to validate things we could've cleaned up ahead of time for a fraction of the cost; we were paying those rates longer than we should have since there was so much to untangle.

It was like getting hit with interest, late fees, and penalties on a bill we could have cut in half if we had just planned ahead.

Abraham Lincoln said, "Give me six hours to chop down a tree, and I will spend the first four sharpening the axe."

Selling Green Mango drove that lesson home. We didn't really start sharpening until year 10, when the offers we were fielding and multiples we were seeing made it clear selling was the right move. Knowing what I know now, I would have started preparing on day one. You always need to have an exit plan. You need to build to sell early. And if you ask James, three is the magic number. While mortgage lenders look at two years of your financials, buyers look at three. That's why it's best to start preparing for the process three years out by having your financials clean as a whistle. Instead, he worked around the clock to help clean up a decade of messes in record time.

With the right prep, we could've closed in half the time *and* walked away with more.

But forget theory. This chapter is tactical. It's about the exact things we *finally* started doing, some too late to fully cash in on, but not too late to learn from.

Start building on them now, no matter where you are in your journey, because when it comes to building to sell, better late than never isn't a meaningless cliché—it's the difference between a good exit and a great one.

Having gone through all this the hard way, I now understand the foundational pillars I should have been taking care of all along. Let's break them down.

## Pillar 1: Tidy Up: Get Your Books Surgically Clean

The moment you sign the LOI, a third-party firm will slide your financials under a microscope through a process called quality of earnings.

Tommy warned me QoE would be intense, but I still wildly underestimated how intense it would be. Again, had we been more prepared, it would have been far faster and smoother.

Either way, think of QoE like a home inspection on steroids. Just as a home inspector checks the foundation, tests the wiring, and hunts for leaks, auditors comb through every account, verify every asset, and challenge every expense, unless you already have a few years of audited financials ready to hand over.

In some ways, the buyer is searching for reasons to pay you less. They're often expecting QoE to reveal problems that will save them money. Some are even banking on it.

A few years ago, I was on the other side of the table, buying a helicopter. During the inspection, our mechanic flagged something seemingly small: A single logbook entry was off.

The seller's records said the engine had just 1,200 hours of flight time left before it needed a full rebuild, but after checking the service logs, we discovered it actually had 1,700 hours left.

In aviation, those 500 hours are a massive difference because helicopter engines have a hard limit. The second you hit the limit, you're on the hook for a rebuild that can cost as much as the aircraft itself.

By our estimates, that one clerical error made the helicopter worth around $600,000 more than the seller's asking price. And by catching what they missed, we captured the margin.

That's exactly how buyers treat your business during QoE. Your mistakes are their margin, and they'll use every single one against you. Every misclassified line item, every commingled expense, every accounting gray area, it's all ammo to negotiate your sale price.

Unlike a helicopter with one logbook, your business has hundreds of entry points that they *can* challenge and *will* challenge.

Accounting errors and outdated financial reporting cost US businesses billions every year.

Most service companies are valued based on a multiple of EBIDTA—your profit before taxes, interest, and accounting tricks. It's the number buyers typically multiply to calculate what your business is worth. I now know the difference between a company that sells for five times EBITDA and one that sells for 10 times, 15 times, or even 20 times often comes down to the quality of its financial records.

Because if your books can't withstand scrutiny, neither will your valuation.

That's why "clean books" doesn't just mean tidy spreadsheets or organized QuickBooks files. When buyers dig in, they're hunting for problems in three specific areas—and if even one is off, your valuation takes a hit:

1. **Proper classification.** Are you treating expenses and assets correctly?
2. **Clear separation.** Is the business truly standalone?
3. **Consistent documentation.** Can you prove every number you claim?

Miss one, and you open the door to renegotiation. Miss two, and they'll slash your valuation. Miss all three, and the deal's probably dead.

## PROPER CLASSIFICATION: ONE TINY OVERSIGHT CAN COST YOU MILLIONS

"Asset or expense?"

It's a boring accounting question until the wrong answer costs you a fortune.

I learned this lesson twice during our exit. Once to our benefit, once not so much. Let's start with the win: rat poison. Specifically, I'm talking about durable plastic bait stations—bait boxes—that look like oversized ant traps for rodents.

You see, most pest control companies sell them as a one-time purchase (if they offer them at all). They sell them, install them, and service them during visits, but the boxes themselves are for the customer to keep.

Why?

Because retrieving them is a hassle. It takes time and coordination, and typically it isn't worth the trouble. At Green Mango, we didn't sell bait boxes like everyone else; we rented them to our customers, turning a one-time sale into monthly recurring revenue.

Since we retrieved the bait boxes after cancellations (to rent them out again), we were able to justify them as assets instead of expenses. At the time of sale, those bait boxes added about $500,000 to our EBITDA. Apply a modest 10× multiple, and that's $5 million in added value, from plastic rectangles I thought less about than the office coffee maker I never touched.

Did I know this going into QoE? Not a chance. But James sure did.

Our termite bait stations were a different story.

We buried those plastic cylinders in customers' yards and never bothered digging them back up. Since we didn't retrieve them, they couldn't qualify as assets. Even if we wanted to reclassify them later, we couldn't unless we were willing to dig them up one by one.

Well, if I could do it over, you'd see me sweating it out in backyards across the Valley, shovel in hand, digging up termite stations like buried treasure.

The payoff would've been worth it.

Termite bait stations are even more common than rodent bait boxes here in Arizona. If we had treated them the same way—rented them and retrieved them—perhaps we could've added another $500,000 in EBITDA, and at least *another* $5 million in sale value, all from another form of plastic we left buried in the dirt.

I learned my lesson: When you misclassify, you don't just lose money—you gift it to the buyer.

But even perfect classification won't save you if your business isn't clearly separated from everything around it. That brings us to the second requirement of clean books: separation.


## CLEAR SEPARATION: KEEP YOUR BUSINESS BOUNDARIES SACRED

Classification tells you what's on your books, while separation tells you what belongs.

Picture it: You're touring your dream home. Perfect kitchen. Stunning bathrooms. Ideal location. Then you open a bedroom door and discover the seller's brother is living there, another bedroom houses their aging parents, and the garage is a full-blown daycare.

"Don't worry, they'll all be gone by the time you move in," the seller insists.

Maybe they will, but now the magic's gone. The trust is gone. And suddenly, you're questioning everything. What's actually part of the deal? What's not? What's hiding behind door number three...and four...and five?

I know the feeling, because this was one of my biggest mistakes with Green Mango.

In my world, everything made perfect sense. Green Mango was our flagship business, but it sat inside a larger ecosystem with multiple sister companies.

Take David, our fleet manager. Technically, he worked for all three companies: Green Mango, Coconut Cleaning, *and* Agave Auto Glass. But his entire salary ran through Green Mango. To us, it was efficient, but to buyers, it was a clear red flag.

"Why are we paying 100 percent for a third of a guy?"

Then there was Hype Pharm, our parent company. It handled HR and accounting across all our businesses. It was logical enough during operations, but during QoE, buyers needed answers. If they bought Green Mango, who would handle HR? Who'd manage the books?

Wait, there was also Hype Pharm The Agency—not to be confused with Hype Pharm the parent company. The Agency was our internal marketing team that served all our businesses.

Green Mango contributed a portion of the budget, so what exactly were buyers getting? A third of our marketing team? A third of David? The whole team? Or none of it?

See the issue?

What made perfect sense in our heads made almost no sense on paper. That's exactly the kind of thing buyers pounce on during QoE—not because they're trying to play "gotcha," but because they need to understand what they're actually buying and what they're not.

When they can't untangle it, they discount it. Or they walk. Even if nothing shady is going on, anything that looks murky will get treated like the risk that it is.

Creating separation after the fact is like trying to separate egg whites from yolks after you've scrambled them—technically possible, but messy, time-consuming, and never fully clean.

Luckily, James had *started* unscrambling eggs when he came aboard. But he hadn't had enough time to unscramble 13 years of mess by the time QoE kicked off. Our lack of clear boundaries cost us all kinds of time, energy, and thousands, maybe millions, in value.

Here's how to maintain separation from day one:

- **Separate legal entities.** Each business should stand on its own.
- **Separate bank accounts.** Never commingle funds between businesses without clear documentation.
- **Use dedicated credit cards.** Each business needs its own financial tools.
- **Draft formal agreements.** Document every shared resource or service.
- **Clarify cost allocations.** If teams or tools are shared, spell out exactly how costs are split.
- **Be careful with personal expenses.** Never run personal costs through business accounts without documentation.

Had we maintained clear separation from day one, we could've closed faster and walked away with more money. After all, buyers don't pay a premium for a house full of squatters.

And even if your classification is perfect and your separation is airtight, buyers still want one last thing: proof that every number you claim is real.


## CONSISTENT DOCUMENTATION: PROVE IT OR LOSE IT

Imagine the home inspector you hired walks into a beautifully finished basement—drywall, lighting, built-ins—but finds out it was all done without permits or records.

It all looks great, but as the homebuyer, you're left wondering if it's up to code. Is it insurable? What happens if it floods? Is any of it under warranty? If so, how would you prove it?

Buyers feel the same way during diligence. Clean numbers and boundaries aren't enough. You need documentation—proof—to back everything up.

It's the difference between "Trust me, bro" and "Here are the receipts."

Which one do you think a buyer will value more?

Despite warnings, the scrutiny still shocked me. Auditors and buyers comb through every line item asking one question: "Can you verify this?" And when I say every line item, I mean every single line item.

Just ask Evan. He was brilliant at driving culture but terrible at keeping receipts. The buyer's team flagged a bunch of charges, including a $217 expense from Raising Cane's.

"What's this for?" they asked.

Evan shrugged. "Chicken."

Technically, he wasn't wrong. But that's not what buyers want to hear. They want documentation, clarity, and confidence. They didn't know whether Evan was feeding the crew or catering his cousin's wedding.

And it wasn't just food. They treated every locker, truck, and office chair like those built-ins in the basement.

"When was it installed? Who paid for it? Where's the proof?"

If we couldn't produce a receipt or a clear record, it became a question mark, and in the world of acquisitions, question marks kill confidence and value.

Think of documentation like filing your taxes and QoE like a guaranteed audit.

You wouldn't claim $1.2 million in business expenses and expect the IRS to take your word for it. You'd gather every receipt, track every deduction, and label every charge because you know the audit is coming.

Let me put it another way: No documentation = no credit. Buyers want paper trails. Wouldn't you?

They want:

- **Tax returns** that match your internal reports
- **Payroll records** that explain comp and bonuses
- **Invoices** for major expenses
- **Receipts** for minor expenses
- **Bank statements** that verify what's coming in and out
- **Contracts** that clarify who owns what and for how long

At the end of the day, what buyers can't verify, they can't value. And what they can't value, they won't pay for.

For the most part, we had clean numbers, but not always

clean paper trails. That meant extra time, stress, and dollars recreating records we should've had from the start. Trust me, during diligence, the last thing you want to be doing is hunting for a chicken receipt.

You want to be able to say, confidently and immediately, "That's the $217 catering receipt from our all-hands meeting in March. Here's the receipt, the bank record, and the calendar invite. Next question?"

I can't overstate it: If I could do it again, I would have had our books audited annually, at least three years before going to market. That way, there wouldn't be any questions about our numbers.

## Pillar 2: Tighten Up: Go to School Before You Go to Market

Most founders think they already know what buyers want.

I knew I didn't.

Before we ever "listed" Green Mango, I spent two full years doing something few probably realize is even an option: I went to school.

I didn't go to college, but my version of going to school is like a practice SAT or ACT before you officially go to market. You simulate the real thing to see where you stand, and if you like your score, you take the plunge and take the test. If not, you go back, study the right sections, and retake it when you're ready. Or better yet, think of it like college athletes working out for professional scouts in the offseason. If they get a first-round grade, they enter the draft to go pro. If not, they return to school to strengthen their weaknesses.

Only in this case, it's not a classroom or basketball court. It's Zooms, boardrooms, and calls and email threads with potential buyers, like private equity firms and strategic acquirers (companies expanding by acquisition) asking what your business is worth *and* what's driving that valuation.

That's what going to school looked like for me.

Armed with nothing more than a clean P&L and a basic pitch deck, buyers could give me rough valuation ranges, real feedback, and clear signals about what they wanted and valued without me handing over full-blown audited financials or anything resembling the rigor of QoE. In some cases, they even gave me official indications of interest (IOIs), which precede LOIs.

I didn't love what I saw, so I asked questions.

"Why a 10× multiple and not 14?"

"What's holding that number back?"

"What would push it higher?"

That's when the real insights started flowing.

Buyers told me what excited them, what scared them, what they'd pay a premium for, and what they'd never value no matter how much I invested.

For example, they love streamlined processes. Think clean org charts, clear pay structures, and predictable meeting rhythms. If your business runs like a machine, your multiple will reflect it. That's not to say they won't buy the business if things aren't dialed in, but the more turnkey it feels, the better.

The process was like asking a real estate agent what buyers want *before* remodeling your home.

Imagine spending $20,000 building a home office only to learn buyers prefer a fourth bedroom—and all it took to transform that office into one was a simple set of French doors.

I wasn't pretending to sell. I was selling. I just wasn't willing to sell for less than what I believed the business was worth, and once I started asking the right people, I didn't have to guess what it was worth or how to get there.

Neither do you.

Do a little research. Figure out who's acquiring businesses in your space, then reach out. Most buyers will take the call because they're in the business of buying businesses.

That's the value of going to school before you go to market: picking up the phone to gather real-time market intel from the people who'll eventually write the checks, and shaping your business into the one they'll pay a premium for. Why guess what buyers want in your business when you can just ask?

## GRADUATION = BRINGING IN A BROKER

If going to school showed me where to improve, then hiring a broker helped me showcase those improvements to the market the right way.

Some founders wait until after they get LOIs. Some never hire a broker at all. For me, the timing was obvious: Buyers had started reaching out to *me*—not the other way around—and market multiples were soaring in real time. I didn't want to just sell; I wanted to maximize the opportunity by maximizing our exposure.

A good broker is like a world-class real estate agent. They know who's serious, who's bluffing, and how to bring more qualified buyers to the table. However, the great ones do more than that. They also help you, the founder, impress the buyers, so that betting on your business is a no-brainer.

Our broker, Brian, gave me a crash course in what buyers actually want to see and hear from founders:

- **Know your numbers cold**. Would you pay a premium for a Ferrari from someone who couldn't even open the hood? Most founders know EBITDA and revenue (as they should), but few can comfortably rattle off LTV, CAC, retention, and reservice rate. When I did, I watched buyers' eyes light up.

- **Show them you're not the business**. As we covered in Chapter 3 on systems, any hint of key-man risk is like buyer repellent. Nothing scares them off faster than a business that hinges on the one person trying to sell it.
- **Keep your cool**. Just like a team reflects its coach, your company reflects your composure. And as we've established throughout this book, business is the ultimate pressure cooker.

It all paid off: We started this process getting multiple ranges of 10 to 14 times EBITDA. By the end, we sold for well above that because we had a business that buyers were willing to pay a premium for.

## COCONUT CLEANING WENT TO SCHOOL, TOO

Evan had a front-row seat to everything we went through selling Green Mango. Plus, he was pulled into the process throughout. Instead of waiting for his own time to come with Coconut, he started transforming the business right then—building to sell early, like I wish I had from day one.

He began with several of the exact changes our potential buyers had flagged.

He added inspection-tracking software that documented exactly which technician performed which service and when. He audited every software subscription and slashed from 31 tools down to 11. He called every vendor to eliminate overlap: discovering, for example, that their existing CRM already included a full phone system. That allowed him to cut a redundant dedicated platform and instantly save $100,000.

He even restructured the team. After realizing they were overstaffed by 15 techs—based on models he'd seen buyers run and questions he'd heard them ask—he made the tough but necessary changes to deliver what buyers want: efficiency.

Those changes alone easily had a six-figure impact on the business. Tack on a multiple, and we're talking about a seven-figure swing in sale price.

Most importantly, Evan started asking himself variations of the same questions I was fielding. Questions about routing, billing, service contracts, and more. He put the whole operation under a microscope as any buyer would.

In other words, Evan went to school too. "Watching Green Mango go through this process was like getting a free MBA," he told me later. "If I'd been asked the same questions, I wouldn't have had answers. Now I do."

However, there's one lesson school can't teach: what happens *after* you sign the LOI and choose your buyer.

## Pillar 3: Level Up: Slam the Accelerator All the Way to Close

The water had receded, but the damage remained.

Imagine that a storm rolled in overnight and flooded that fictional basement just hours before the final walkthrough.

The beautiful finished space that helped sell the house has turned into a disaster zone. Puddles of murky water sit still, inviting mold to form. Ruined carpet squishes underfoot. Black water lines stain the drywall where the flood peaked. The sump pump hums faintly in the corner—too little, too late. You stare at the wall, half-expecting it to crumble.

Then your phone buzzes. It's your realtor.

"The buyers will be there in 30 minutes," she says, tension in her voice. "I have to disclose the flooding."

Your stomach drops. Months of prep, paperwork, and back-and-forth is all on the verge of collapse thanks to six inches of water at the worst possible time.

Forget the past. All the buyer sees now is the damage right in front of them.

The home they fell in love with months ago no longer exists. Best case, they command a steep discount. Worst case, they walk away entirely. Either way, you can already feel the money slipping through your fingers.

Just like in real estate, the last impression matters as much as the first impression.

That last impression is what buyers call TTM—your Trailing Twelve Months of financial performance. Buyers typically apply a multiple to your TTM profits to firm up your sale price as QoE winds down.


## TTM IS A MOVING WINDOW

The buyer's initial offer is typically based on your most recent 12 months of profits (specifically, your monthly EBITDA margins). But most deals, as we've established, take two to four months to close on the conservative end.

That's another quarter of financials to consider.

Others, like ours, can take even more than a quarter or two from LOI to close. Either way, by close, the window will have moved. Your TTM will have shifted, and your sale price *could* shift with it.

If your profits stay steady or improve during this window, your sale price can hold or even climb with your EBITDA. But if they slip? So can the offer. Sometimes catastrophically. No buyer is paying full price for what appears to be a sinking ship.

In our case, we maintained consistent performance throughout most of our six-month sale process, which secured our original valuation. Looking back, I realize we missed a massive opportunity to intentionally create and capitalize on upward momentum.

Remember that record-breaking 38 percent profit margin we hit in July (while I was in Thailand)?

Had I incentivized my team to maintain that level of performance through October, according to my math, our valuation could have soared by about $30 million.

I knew we were going to grow as we went through the process, which is why I requested a fixed multiple on EBITDA instead of a fixed sales price. They pushed back, and I didn't.

It's one thing I wish I had negotiated more strongly on. If it were the opposite, a record dip in profits during the process, we both know the buyer would have made me pay for it, as any buyer should.

When it was all said and done, we increased our EBITDA by almost $400,000 in that TTM window. Given our premium multiple, well, you can do the math on how much money we left on the table. I don't want to. It hurts too much.

This is why, if I could do it again, I wouldn't just *maintain* performance; I'd incentivize my team to *accelerate* it during that critical window between offer and closing. In turn, I would have pushed harder for a multiple based on our TTM of EBITDA instead of a fixed sales price when the offer we accepted first materialized.

Lesson learned.

## TIE THEIR BONUS TO YOUR BUYOUT

I'd sit my leadership team down and say it plainly: "We're preparing to sell—and your performance directly impacts our final price."

Then I'd put real money behind those words.

I'd align their incentives with our final push by offering them a slice of the upside they helped create. In practical terms, I'd reward them for every percentage point of EBITDA above our expected baseline during that sale window. And by doing so, I would have been far more confident pushing for a sale price based on real-time EBITDA, as opposed to a fixed price.

Simply put, your team shares a set percentage of any value they create *above* the projected sale price.

If you want to implement this in your own business, here's the formula:

1. Set your projected EBITDA (your baseline).
2. Offer your team a cut (say, 20 percent) of every dollar above your projected EBITDA.
3. Divide the bonus pool based on role and impact.

Let's say your projected EBITDA is $5 million, and the buyer offers a 10× multiple. Your projected sale price is $50 million ($5 million × 10 = $50 million).

If your team lifts EBITDA from $5 million to $6 million, that $1 million boost could add $10 million to your sale price ($6 million × 10 = $60 million).

Your team gets 20 percent of that $10 million, so they split $2 million, while you take home an extra $8 million.

When your CFO stands to earn $500,000 from that bonus pool, do you think he scrutinizes expenses differently? When your operations director could make $400,000 by improving efficiency, does she tolerate waste?

You already know the answer.

When your team's financial future is directly tied to the company's performance during the sale window, every-thing changes. Suddenly, EBITDA isn't just an acronym your leadership team cares about. It becomes a scoreboard everyone watches obsessively.

They sharpen their focus, chase profit, cut dead weight, question everything, and perform like the outcome depends on it, because now it does.

# HOW SHARP IS YOUR AXE?

Ask yourself these three questions to see how exit-ready you really are:

## Are Your Books So Clean a Buyer Can't Poke Holes?

Do you have proper classification, separation, and documentation? If your books are already clean, get them audited in advance (it's worth it). If not, start working on your hygiene.

Unverified numbers are like Monopoly money.

Like I said before, aim to start annual audits at least three years before selling. The earlier you begin, the more credibility and leverage you'll have when it counts.

## Have You Actually Asked What Buyers Want?

Have you met with strategics and private equity firms? Do you know where you stand and what they truly value? Have you shaped your business to reflect what the market rewards? Go to school before you go to market.

## Are Your Numbers Trending Up?

How's your TTM—especially your EBITDA margins? Is momentum working for you or against you? Would a buyer say "This company's still growing" or "They've peaked"?

Instead of coasting to the finish line, accelerate through it.

These questions reflect the three core pillars: *Tidy up. Tighten up. Level up.*

# PRO TIPS TO MULTIPLY YOUR LEVERAGE

Negotiating a multimillion-dollar deal for the business you built is not for the faint of heart. Below are a few strategies and shifts to consider to help you win the deal you want.

## Know Your Number

$10 million isn't $10 million. Do the post-tax, post-debt math before you make a decision. When I sold Green Mango, I calculated exactly what needed to hit my account to change my family's life, not just create a different set of problems. If a $10 million offer means $6 million in your pocket, but you know you need to make $8 million on the deal, you'll know to walk. That clarity gave me power. It helped me turn down offers others would've taken and accept the right one without second-guessing. Know your number before someone else names theirs.

## Price Your Business Like a Buyer Would

Most service businesses are valued using a simple formula: TTM EBITDA × multiple = valuation. For pest control, that multiple ranged from 10× to 14× when we sold. In broader home services, 3× to 7× is more typical. That means an HVAC business earning $1 million in EBITDA might sell for $3 to $7 million—not the $20 million the owner's dreaming of. However, not all buyers prioritize the same metrics.

- A financial buyer (like a private equity firm) almost always focuses on EBITDA—they want profitability and predictability.
- A strategic buyer (like Orkin or Terminix) may be more interested in top-line revenue, especially if they're acquiring to gain market share, enter a new region, or cross-sell services.

But even in strategic deals, EBITDA is still key. A strong profit engine drives higher multiples, greater interest, and a smoother exit. Realistic expectations prevent painful disappointments and help you focus on the levers you can actually pull to increase your valuation.

## Be Passionately Detached

Famed negotiator Chester Karrass titled one of his best-selling books *In Business As In Life—You Don't Get What You Deserve, You Get What You Negotiate.* The most powerful place to negotiate from is detachment. I got the deal of the century and everything I asked for because I didn't need it. I could walk away, and I would have. That posture gave me power. It took me a long time to believe it, but what finally got me there was the idea Mark taught me along the way and I mentioned in Chapter 2 on mindset: "Everything always works out." That belief gave me peace, and that peace gave me leverage. When you don't need the deal, you hold all the cards.

## Build Your Personal Brand While You Build Your Business

A few years ago, I Googled myself. The first thing that popped up was a photo of me holding a fish. I hated that picture because it felt like the internet was telling the wrong story about me. I had no control. It made me look like a die-hard fisherman, which I wasn't. What story is the internet telling about you? The way I see it, you're an asset just like your company, and your personal brand is like a baseball card; it showcases your stats before you walk in the room. The right personal brand builds credibility, attracts buyers, and opens doors long after you close the deal. So get out there. Try podcasting, writing, or speaking. Focus on building your social media following. Consider hiring a PR consultant. See if you can become a go-to resource when local news outlets need an expert in your field. Potential buyers will definitely Google you, so make sure they find the right stuff. I believe the right story can lead to the kind of trust and credibility that can generate higher multiples from the jump. Either way, don't wait: Take control of the narrative now.

## Lawyer Up

Some buyers aren't buyers; they're *browsers*—peeking under your hood to poach your people, process, or IP. You're opening the data room. Make sure the right locks are in place. Get a premium lawyer, bulletproof your NDAs, and protect your time, team, and trade secrets. I've heard of founders losing team members, tech, and leverage by treating NDAs like after-thoughts.

## The Sooner You Start, the Smoother the Finish

Even if you're years from selling, going through this preparation process transforms you as an operator. Twelve months after implementing these pillars, Green Mango would have been more profitable, more efficient, and more valuable, even if we hadn't sold. That's why I considered doubling down instead of moving on. The discipline of building to sell creates the kind of business you actually enjoy running, one with clean books, clear boundaries, and consistent growth. In some ways, the process itself is the reward.

# BEGIN WITH THE END IN MIND

They aren't always linear, but together, the three pillars of a premium exit sharpen your business into an asset buyers are happy to pay a premium for.

And remember, exit is just one spoke of the Value Vortex.

Even with a perfect exit score, a low score on any other spoke can drag your valuation down.

Though it's the final spoke in the Vortex, every spoke multiplies, or undermines, the others. Put differently, they're all connected.

Start sharpening your axe today—whether an exit is years away or right around the corner.

By focusing on these three pillars now, you'll accomplish two things at once:

You'll build a business that runs better today and one that sells for more tomorrow. You'll win now *and* later.

## Chapter Summary

- Selling your business is like selling your house: The best time to prep is long before you list.
- Clean books sell businesses. Get your financials surgically clean—correct classifications, consistent documentation, no commingling, and ideally, three years of audited records.
- Tailor your business to what buyers want. Go to school before you go to market by connecting with buyers in your space to understand what they value.
- Keep performance trending up. Your trailing 12 months (TTM) can make or break your valuation. Consider incentivizing your team by giving them a set percentage of any value they create *above* the projected sale price during that TTM period.
- Start exit prep long before you plan to leave. Buyers pay most for businesses that run well without the owner.

# ELEVEN
# LETTING GO



*"Legacy is not leaving something for people. It's leaving something in people."*
– Peter Strople

I led Green Mango for 735 Tuesdays.

On my final Tuesday, I stood in front of a room packed with people I loved, trying not to fall apart.

"Can everyone hear me?" Evan's voice bounced off the concrete walls, barely cutting through the buzz. The sun was just starting to rise. The griddle let out a soft hiss as the last few pancakes hit the heat, lost in the steady swell of noise. The team didn't know it yet, but I'd already flipped my last batch for good.

Rows of couches bled into rows of folding chairs, all aimed at the projector like pews on Easter morning. Every chair was full, including the extras we'd set out that morning. Stragglers stood shoulder to shoulder, packed like sardines behind the very last row. On the far wall, our KPIs and core values hung like championship banners. I saw them now as bold reminders of how far we'd come.

The projector flickered to life. Evan slid the mic from its stand. "Okay then," he said with a grin. "Let's kick this thing off with a bang!"

Kathleen, our HR director, stepped up to the mic like she had dozens of times before. She smiled as her eyes moved across the room. "We've got a few new faces in the room today..." she began, her voice warm and welcoming. As always, she started with birthdays. Work anniversaries and customer shoutouts would follow. Even our meetings had a rhythm to them now. As she called out the first birthday, the room erupted. Cheers, clapping, and voices piled on top of each other.

All that for a birthday, I thought.

I expected the clapping, the smiles, and a few hoots and hollers. Our team genuinely cared about each other, and it showed. You could see it before the meeting officially started in the hugs, the high-fives, and the back pats. Observing it made me swell with pride. Techs from both branches, some meeting for the first time, chopping it up like old friends over breakfast.

Then came the second name. Louder. By the third, Kathleen had to pause, completely drowned out by the sound. She smiled, waited, tried again. But the roar didn't let up.

You know that moment when a speaker tries to talk but the crowd won't let them? That's exactly what happened—after just one name. Even with the mic cranked, Kathleen couldn't cut through the noise.

She had to stop and wait it out after every birthday, every anniversary, and every shoutout. It felt more like a rock concert than a staff meeting. In all my years in business, I'd never experienced anything like that. And the craziest part is, not a single person in the room knew what was coming. To them, this was *normal*. This was Green Mango.

A few years earlier, that same Green Mango was a revolving door. Back then, even doubling a barista's pay wasn't enough to convince them to join us. Our culture wasn't bad, but it certainly wasn't this. It was just...normal. Expected. Ordinary. Now, people were lining up to join our team, and once they were here, they never wanted to leave. I felt it too. Even after 14 years of grinding, the only thing that could pull me away was an offer I truly couldn't refuse.

Kathleen joined the company around that time. She had a front row seat to every hard change I'd fought to make, and she saw it all—the hiring, the firing, the cheating, the lying. The broken promises. The tough conversations. The slow, uphill climb to shift our culture that felt impossible at times. Now she was witnessing the payoff. She was feeling it in that room, just like I was. Unlike the audience, she knew what was coming. While the team roared around her, she caught my eye and shot a quick wink. I'll never forget that quiet, knowing gesture, because it broke the dam.

I blinked fast. Swallowed hard. My chest tightened. I glanced left, then right—and quietly slipped away. I ducked into my office, leaned against the door, and broke down. I'm not a crier. Heck, I'm not even that emotional, but I cried more in that moment, alone in my office, than I think I had in all 36 years of my life.

Meanwhile, the applause outside kept rolling. The walls practically shook as Kathleen had to battle just to make it through her shoutouts.

And yet not long ago, these same walls were silent.

When Evan introduced "counterpart shoutouts" to help me drive better culture, three straight manager meetings ended in crickets. Picture folded arms and blank stares. No one had anything nice to say about their teammates, so they said nothing at all.

That silence, which gutted me, told me everything I needed to know.

I bought out Dusty around that same time. In doing so, I bet millions I didn't have—on *myself*. No more cofounder. No one to split the pressure of payroll. No one to trade war stories with at 2 am. No one to shoulder the load when it got too heavy to carry alone.

The buyout felt more like a divorce than a business deal. We butted heads like brothers, but we built this thing together. Losing him hurt more than I let on.

Now it was just me, a balloon payment I couldn't afford, and a team depending on me to not screw it up. Overnight, I felt the full weight of the business drop onto my shoulders.

My dad's early investment had nearly broken me, and that was just one man's faith. Now I carried the weight of mortgages, car payments, braces, and college funds all on my own.

This wasn't a two-man operation anymore. We'd built a beautiful monster. Multiple departments. Hundreds of employees. Thousands of customers. Real families. Real livelihoods. Real consequences if I failed.

By then, I'd already turned down multiple eight-figure offers. Sometimes I surprised myself with how fast I said no. Other times, I'd lie awake wondering if I'd made a massive mistake. What made me think I could carry all of this? What if I were the reason it would all come crashing down?

If it didn't work out, to quote my old white whale John, I'd be "done."

So I did what I'd always done when my back hit the wall: I pushed harder. In a pinch, I answered phones. I knocked on doors. Not because we needed the sales, but because I felt the team needed to see their leader in the trenches. They needed to see what was possible. What they didn't know was that I was paying incentives out of my personal savings just to keep my word and to keep the fire lit. Instead of role-playing until 2 am like Dusty and I used to, Evan and I were whiteboarding in my family room, solving problems no one else was even aware of.

We rolled out KPIs not just as goals but as visible, inescapable targets. The seven-week rotation became an expectation. We hit those 38 percent profit margins. We added millions to the bottom line and top line—as a team. While I worked like it was day one all over again, Lyss held our family together. I'd raid our savings to make payroll, and she'd just squeeze my hand. She never got upset. She never even asked me to slow down or take a beat even when she had every reason to.

Evan, Kait, James S., James C., Joe, Gustavo, Kathleen. From managers to techs, everyone had to step up, and some had to go. We didn't clean house, but we unearthed skeletons I didn't even know were there. That's what happens when you open every drawer. When due diligence finally came, it didn't spark our evolution. It extended it. It took everything up *another* notch.

Betting on myself was when Green Mango began evolving into what I saw that morning.

For the first time ever, our entire company stood under one roof. A sea of charcoal and green. Polos. Hats. Smiles. Hugs. High-fives. A hundred and fifty people who were as much friends as they were co-workers.

I saw CSRs I'd hired straight out of high school who had grown into total professionals. Sales reps who'd left everything behind to relocate. Techs who started by shadowing routes and were now leading entire teams. They'd built careers here, bought homes, started families, and climbed out of debt. Some had even met their spouses through Green Mango.

Outside, the parking lot overflowed with flat-black trucks. Clean. No dents, no scratches. Lyss had rolled up just before the meeting started and couldn't help but record the surreal sight. In 2015, I took a picture of 25 service trucks lined up in a lot. Then I saved that picture in my journal along with this exact note: "I always dreamed of being this big...but now that we have 25 service trucks, it just seems like a dream."

On this Tuesday morning, we had 150 service trucks packing our parking lot. I was living the dream.

I thought back to the day Dusty and I changed our shirts and marched back into that bank after being denied. We couldn't even get a loan for that first additional truck. Every truck after that was a visual milestone I celebrated in private. And now we had 150? Pinch me. Heck, even our *trucks* had a manager now.

The one thing uniting all of it was Green Mango. But really, it was *me*. And in a few minutes, I was going to tell them I was leaving. Leaving them. Leaving it. Leaving for good. Just when I saw it so clearly. Evan, Kait, James S., James C., Joe, Gustavo—I'm sure they all saw it. I know Kathleen did. I did it. *We* did it. Everybody in that room felt like family. To them, this was just another Tuesday, just business as usual.

To me, it was the most bittersweet feeling ever.

The 22-year-old kid who started this company was gone. He was 145 pounds soaking wet, fresh off his mission, dating his dream girl. He had no experience, no safety net, no plan beyond knocking on doors. Just a truck, a partner, and a dream that felt too big for his body.

Now I was 36. A husband, a father of two. In that kid's place stood a man who'd learned to bet everything (including money he didn't have) on the only thing he could control: himself.

Green Mango was my firstborn. It was all my actual kids

had ever known. It was all Lyss and I had ever known. It was born before we got married. This business didn't just change my life—it was my life. It built me as much as I built it.

And now I was about to let it go?

Truth be told, the deal wasn't even done. Just eight hours earlier, I had still been on the phone with PestCo's managing director and our point of contact, waiting on one last signature at the 11th hour.

"There's no way we're not closing," he had assured me.

But what if we didn't? What if I dropped the bomb only to show up tomorrow like nothing happened?

The team didn't know their potential new bosses were already in the room. They just saw the usual slew of guests we often welcomed in to learn from us. Imagine that: Others were now learning from *us*. Our shop tours had become nearly as legendary as the ones I used to attend to learn from Tommy.

After pouring everything into this company—my money, my marriage, my sanity—for the first time in 14 years, I felt selfish, even guilty, almost like I was hiding something.

What would the team think when I told them? Would they feel abandoned, betrayed, resentful? Or would they understand? Maybe they'd feel all of it at once, the same way I did.

But how could I tell them to be excited, that this was a good thing, when I could barely hold back my own tears? What if I said the wrong thing? What if someone stood up mid-speech and stormed out? What if others then followed suit?

That had happened to PestCo before. Even with better benefits, more time off, and extra resources, they warned me: *Prepare for the worst.*

Meanwhile, this wasn't just a business I was selling. It was my identity. A piece of my purpose. The very thing that had shaped every decision, every sacrifice, every victory for nearly half of my life.

How do you say goodbye to something like that? How do you explain to 150 people that you're walking away from the thing that brought you all together? How do you distill 14 years into four measly presentation slides?

It seemed like just yesterday that we had been scraping for customer reviews, lucky to find a few worth sharing. Even when I knew we were building something special, there were times it felt like I was the only one who could see it. Those moments made me question if any of it was actually working.

These days, the list of five-star reviews was so long we had to cut it in half. Kathleen couldn't just rattle them off like an auctioneer. She had to pause between the applause, let the claps die down, let the weight of those words settle.

I never went to college, but I imagine this is what it feels like to send your kid off. That last warm hug in the driveway. The lump in your throat. Desperately wanting to hold them, squeeze them, for just one more second. You'd give anything to go back. You'd happily relive the worst of times if it meant more time with them. You realize, in that moment, it all went too fast. They don't need you anymore. Maybe they don't even want you anymore, but you'll worry sick about them for the rest of your life. Sadly, you can't stop time. And now, it's time to let them go.

Lyss compared it to sending your kid on a mission, only this time, you know they're not coming back.

You know it's good and you know it's right, but that doesn't make it any easier. You raised them. Loved them. Grew with them. Bled for them. And now, you're just standing there, staring at taillights, blinking hard against tears.

It felt like we were giving away our firstborn.

I took a deep breath, wiped my eyes, and straightened my shirt. That moment right there perfectly captured the entrepreneurial journey. You toughen up. You put on a happy face. You become the beacon when no one else can. You carry pressure no one else can see. You learn to stay steady—not too high, not too low—because the highs are dizzying and the lows can break you. You chew glass in silence for the greater good.

Just like that, when I finally felt like I'd made it, the time had come to let go. I pulled myself together. Put on the same happy face I'd worn a million times before. I reminded myself that this was mission accomplished. And that the team needed to feel my excitement for the next chapter, not my sadness for closing the book.

I walked to the front of the room as Kathleen wrapped up. She handed me the mic as the screen lit up with Maya Angelou's words: "To know where you're going, you must understand where you've been."

We started with the history of Green Mango.

I shared the revenue over the years—a rising bar chart that filled me with pride, but it couldn't even begin to capture 90 percent of what I wanted to say. Much of it was invisible. The nights, the doubts, the sacrifices, the stress, the highs and the lows. Most of it they'd never know. Even this book barely scratches the surface.

I told the team the story you already know—the one from Dutch Bros. The moment my mission shifted from money to meaning. Then I pulled up our original Scope of Service. It was identical to today's, with the same promises and same standards. Flat-black trucks, uniformed techs, pet-safe products, even our scorpion-free guarantee. We were premium from day one, even when we couldn't afford to be.

Next slide: A grainy photo appeared of me and my dad, 14 years ago, in his office at Falcon Field where it all began.

I looked down at the floor, searching for words while hiding my face. I couldn't meet his eyes—not with him sitting right there in the row of guests.

When my parents divorced, I was convinced I'd never see him again. Hot tears streamed down my red, three-year-old cheeks when they broke the news. That fear of losing my father forever is my first memory. I don't remember much from that age, but I remember that day.

He knelt beside me, his hand on my shoulder, his wet eyes locked on mine. "You'll see me every Tuesday, son," he said, his voice steady. "Be outside at five. I'll never be late."

Seconds later, he was gone. I watched his taillights fade into the distance.

But he kept his promise. Every single week, rain or shine. Even when he had nothing to say. Even when I acted like I didn't care. Not once did I walk outside and find an empty driveway.

And my father was never just on time; he was always early. He rolled up every Tuesday at 4:58 pm on the dot for more than 14 years straight. That's 735 Tuesdays in a row.

That's what commitment looks like. That's what stuck with me.

Fast forward 19 years.

I was 22 years old, standing in that same office on the screen—*his* office—asking him to invest in a pest control company that didn't exist yet.

"My dad loves aviation," I said, voice cracking. "He passed that love on to me. And that chair he's sitting in?" I pointed to the photo. "That's the chair where Dusty and I pitched him on Green Mango."

The money I was asking for could've paid for my college tuition. It could've been saved, invested, or spent on literally anything safer than two kids with no experience, no savings, and no plan beyond knocking on doors during a recession.

We didn't have a pitch deck. We didn't even have a single slide. My dad's business partner rightfully ran for the hills.

I looked out at the team, locked eyes with my dad, then pointed to my younger self on the screen. "I probably didn't give him a return on capital...because I didn't even know what that meant at the time."

But I was arrogant enough to make two promises:

"We're going to build the biggest pest control company in Arizona."

I paused.

"And it'll be the best investment you ever make."

Back then, I didn't know what return on capital meant, or anything about finance. I barely knew what a slide deck was. I certainly didn't know how to create one. But I understood commitment. I knew how to keep a promise, because Dad had been showing me how since I was three years old.

And when he said yes, it wasn't because I was his son. It was because I had a *history of keeping my word.*

That history didn't start with Green Mango.

I committed to Scouts and earned my Arrow of Light, then went on to earn the rank of Eagle Scout. I committed to aviation, and I earned my pilot's license shortly after my driver's license. Then I racked up three more ratings by the age of 19. I completed a two-year mission in Canada working seven days a week—no phone, no paycheck, no breaks. Just a promise to serve and a commitment to see it through.

But I also quit. Once.

In high school, I walked off the basketball court mid-game. Frustrated with my coach, I quit for real. The next day, we met. He wanted me back, but he felt he had to send a message to the team: I wouldn't start another game for the rest of the season. He kept his promise. I never did start again.

It was both humiliating and exactly what I needed. It reinforced what my dad had shown me all along: Once you commit, you can't quit.

Since then, I haven't quit anything. And trust me, I've wanted to.

I didn't love spraying houses, but I did it anyway. For years. I didn't love rejection, but I knocked doors anyway. For years. I didn't love Maricopa, but I drove there anyway. For years, without fail. I didn't love late payroll, tough conversations, angry customers, or sleepless nights, but I kept showing up—for 14 straight years.

Because that's what commitment looks like.

Sure, my dad said yes to investing in Green Mango, but more than that, he said yes to *me*.

By the time I pitched him, my history of keeping my word spoke louder than any slide ever could.

I looked around the room—150 people strong—with pure admiration and amazement. Green Mango hats and shirts from the front to the back, flanked by charcoal and green banners, with the packed parking lot just outside. It was a visual I'll never unsee.

I saw the pride in their eyes, the love they had for this place. The love they had for each other. It was the kind of camaraderie everyone could feel. I gave myself a moment—that mental hug goodbye. A chance to soak it in one last time, to see what we built, to feel what we built, to let that warm embrace linger just a second longer.

I looked at each manager, fighting back tears. They could feel it, too. It was good, it was right, it was time. But that didn't make it any easier. We'd built something special. The biggest privately-owned pest control business in Arizona. I looked at Lyss—I couldn't have done any of it without her. I wouldn't have survived without her. Then I looked at my dad.

I paused. Collected myself.

After 14 years and 735 Tuesdays, these words echoed in my head:

*We did it, Dad.*

*We did it.*

Then I made it official.

I told the team I was stepping down and PestCo was stepping in. PestCo brought better benefits thanks to deeper pockets and national backing, more paid time off than I could ever afford, even a real commitment to fair pay—one of the final sticking points I required in our negotiations. Green Mango was in good hands. They were in good hands. It was time for me to let go.

I even joked, "They have a much bigger bank account than I do."

They still do.

I came home to a wall of hand-drawn posterboards and balloons (charcoal and green, of course).

"Congrats, babe."

"We're so proud of you."

"Welcome to the one percent."

Banks drew a Green Mango truck with a spray rig and all. Ivory filled her posterboards with hearts. Photos from every chapter of our journey lined the walls. I saw my life before my eyes. I saw myself growing up, our family growing up. The kids in tiny Green Mango shirts at two and three years old. Lyss and me in the early days, two kids just figuring it out.

There were pictures I hadn't seen in years that stopped me in my tracks. I paused in the hallway, taking it in. Then letting go. Nothing changed, like I told the team. Life moved on for them and for me. My kids will miss the snacks and the swag we always had at the office, and they'll miss the team, too. Some were like family to them. But something deeper stayed with me. I didn't realize it then, but the first lesson in building to sell, and really building any business for that matter, didn't come from a mentor, a book, or a customer. It came from my dad...one Tuesday at a time.

Because that's all a business really is: a series of promises. To your customers, to your team, to yourself.

You don't win by being the smartest or the luckiest. You win by keeping your word.

Perhaps the ultimate validation of everything came quietly after my announcement: Not one person quit that day. Nobody wanted to leave Green Mango. Their commitment spoke louder than any multiple ever could.

On top of that, they were genuinely happy for me. The room had erupted in cheers when I made the announcement. It was everything I hoped for and then some. It was like my version of the Waste Management's 16th hole that morning. At that point, the techs were the people I knew the least. They were on routes instead of in the office. Still, several pulled me aside that morning. One even said, "I couldn't believe you didn't sell sooner." All of them were truly happy for me.

Lyss, my dad, and I took a teary-eyed photo in the warehouse before leaving, one last goodbye while PestCo walked the team through the transition. Before I pulled away, I cruised slowly through the lot one more time, looking at what I'd built. At what *we'd* built. I'll never forget seeing all those trucks lined up. I drove away proud, knowing my baby was in good hands.

When you build to sell, you don't just accept an offer. You choose the buyer as much as they choose you. And I chose one that I knew would take care of my people.

Now I'm making new promises. To my wife, to my kids, to myself. Promises I plan to keep.

So yes, Green Mango sold for a record multiple. It grew into the biggest privately-owned pest control provider in Arizona. It really was the best investment my dad ever made. But what I'm most proud of is this: I said we'd do it, and we did.

Days later, Lyss and I drove past the office for the first time since the acquisition. I blinked fast, staring out the window. When I glanced over, her eyes were wet too.

I cracked a smile. "I didn't know you liked Green Mango so much."

She looked over at me with a soft smile on her face.

"I didn't know you did either."

I used to think success meant a big house, a private jet, or a certain number in the bank. But real success? It's something else entirely. It's the feeling of being genuinely happy with your choices and achievements, regardless of external measures.

The wire transfer was a thrill when it finally went through, but that didn't make me successful. Because success wasn't in the number—it was in what the number represented.

The business didn't just make me money; it built me. It transformed that 22-year-old kid into someone who could carry the weight of hundreds of families, someone who could keep promises that seemed impossible. I can fly now—literally. I take my helicopter up whenever I want. I can toss on my dad hat far more often now. If I wanted to break my phone, I really could. Maybe I will after we sell Coconut.

And now? The people who matter most don't want my money. They want my time.

Banks and Ivory would choose five more minutes on the trampoline over another $100,000 in the family trust. Lyss asked them and they confirmed. Lyss would too. Every time.

I can't count how many times I chose work over family, but somehow, we made it work. Banks sat in on meetings and listened to every podcast. I told him everything I could to shatter any self-limiting beliefs early, the way this journey had shattered mine. Ivory loved the people, the energy. She's dreaming big now too.

But if it came down to CEO Cameron or father Cameron, which version do you think they'd choose?

Exactly.

Which version would your family choose?

If you're somewhere between the dream and the break-through, keep going.

Maybe you're still in your version of Maricopa. Maybe you're still knocking on doors—literally or metaphorically—wondering if it'll ever pay off. I've been there. And I can tell you: It is worth it. But not just for the reasons you think. You're not only building a business; you're building yourself.

You won't build to sell by copying me. But you *will* by building systems that don't need you, teams that thrive without you, and a life you actually want to keep living when the work is done.

This book is simple because that's what I wish I had back then. However, simple isn't easy. This journey was anything but.

We put everything into Green Mango, and we got out exactly what we put in. But if there's one thing I hope you take from all this, it's not that I made it.

It's that *you* can too.

If you stay consistent, keep your word, and don't stop, you'll get there. That's it. That's the whole secret.

Green Mango wasn't my dream. But it gave me a life I never dreamed was possible.

One Tuesday at a time.

Me pitching Green Mango to my dad

25 Green Mango trucks in 2015

Green Mango co-founder Dusty and me

My bad haircut

Me announcing the merger

Lyss and me on closing day

I've passed my love for
aviation down to Banks

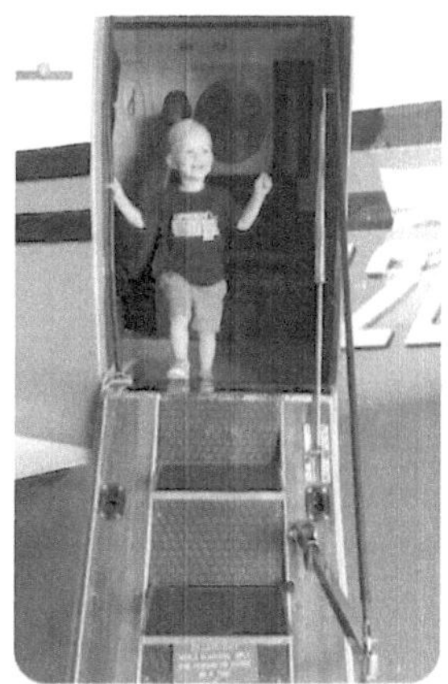

Check out that branding

Ivory and me back in
the day

Ivory and me on Green Mango's eighth birthday

Banks and Ivory in their Green Mango gear

Lyss holding Banks

← Excited Ivory

An early Green Mango →
holiday card starring Banks

Removing bees in 120-degree heat

Learning how to sell the hard way

# ACKNOWLEDGMENTS

To my kids: I hope you saw the cost. But more than that, I hope you saw the courage. I hope you know that anything worth doing takes *everything* you've got. I wrote this book so you'd know what it took.

To Lyss: You never once asked me to stop chasing this dream even when it cost you time, sleep, and sanity. Thank you for being the glue that holds our family together. And for teaching the kids "Lazy people work twice."

To my mom: I'll never forget the day you left your job at the salon. I'd cracked my head open, you got the call, and your boss wouldn't let you leave. You didn't let him stop you. In fact, you left for good. You turned the first floor into your very own salon just to be with your family. You inspire me, Mom. I'm proud to be following in your footsteps in more ways than one.

To my dad: Thank you. Thank you. Thank you. I don't know what more to say, Dad. Thank you for teaching me. For betting on me. Really, for gambling on me. It means the world to me to have a father like you and to give you everything you gave me back and more.

ENDNOTES

1. "Fire, Fuel, and Second Chances: The Origins of the Hoover Nozzle and Ring Near Brown Field, San Diego, California May 25, 1978," Check-Six.com, accessed July 24, 2025, https://check-six.com/Crash_Sites/N2300H-Hoover-1978.htm.

2. George Bernard Shaw. "Success does not consist in never making mistakes, but in never making the same one a second time," as attributed in various online sources including GoodReads, A-ZQuotes, and BrainyQuote, accessed August 5, 2025.

3. "There Isn't a Man Alive Who Hasn't Made a Mistake," *Sierra Hotel Aeronautics*, October 10, 2018, https://sierrahotel.net/blogs/news/a-life-lesson.

4. Mike Wolfe. "How Many Businesses Reach $1 Million Revenue? The Truth Might Shock You," *Valder Substack*, June 16, 2024, https://valder.substack.com/p/how-many-businesses-reach-1-million.

5. Antoine de Saint-Exupéry. *Wind, Sand and Stars*, trans. Lewis Galantière, Harcourt, 1939 (original French: *Terre des hommes*).

6. "In His Own Words," *The Muhammad Ali Center*, accessed July 24, 2025, https://alicenter.org/meet-ali/in-his-own-words/.

7. U.S. Census Bureau. "Measuring the Effect of COVID-19 on U.S. Small Businesses: The Small Business Pulse Survey, May 2020," https://www2.census.gov/ces/wp/2020/CES-WP-20-16.pdf.

8. Emily Barone. "The Pandemic Forced Thousands of Businesses to Close—But New Ones Are Launching at Breakneck Speed," *Time*, July 22, 2021, https://time.com/6082576/pandemic-new-businesses.

9. Thomas Franck. "Tesla Is the Biggest Short in the U.S. Stock Market," *CNBC*, April 11, 2018, https://www.cnbc.com/2018/04/11/tesla-is-the-biggest-short-in-the-us-stock-market.html.

10. Tom Metcalf and Dana Hull. "Tesla Is Burning Through $6,500 Every Minute," *Yahoo! Finance*, May 2, 2018, https://finance.yahoo.com/news/tesla-burning-6-500-every-115828538.html.

11. Richard Suttmeier. "Tesla Stock May Fall Below Its 'Reversion to the Mean'," *Investopedia*, April 4, 2018, https://www.investopedia.com/news/tesla-stock-may-fall-below-its-reversion-mean/.

12. "Tesla is heading for a cash crunch," *The Economist*, April 5, 2018, https://www.economist.com/business/2018/04/05/tesla-is-heading-for-a-cash-crunch.

13. Steve Kovach. "Elon Musk: Tesla had 'single-digit weeks' as it teetered on brink of collapse," *CNBC*,

November 25, 2018, https://www.cnbc.com/2018/11/25/elon-musk-tesla-had-single-digit-weeks-before-it-would-die.html.

14. "Tesla CEO Elon Musk, stressed but "optimistic," predicts big increase in Model 3 production," *CBS News*, April 13, 2018, https://www.cbsnews.com/news/elon-musk-tesla-model-3-problems-interview-today-2018-04-13/.

15. Lesley Stahl. "Tesla CEO Elon Musk: The 60 Minutes Interview," *CBS News*, December 9, 2018, https://www.cbsnews.com/news/tesla-ceo-elon-musk-the-2018-60-minutes-interview/.

16. Bloomberg. "'Words Fail Me. It's Insanity.' While Elon Musk Loves Tesla's New Tent Factory, Others Aren't So Sure," *Yahoo! Finance*, June 25, 2018, https://finance.yahoo.com/news/apos-words-fail-insanity-apos-124204670.html.

17. Elon Musk. *X* post, June 18, 2018, 10:36 pm, https://x.com/elonmusk/status/1008916455948148736.

18. Andrew J. Hawkins and Sean O'Kane. "Tesla is finally making money on the Model 3," *The Verge*, August 1, 2018, https://www.theverge.com/2018/8/1/17639588/tesla-earning-q2-2018-model-3-production.

19. Walter Isaacson. *Steve Jobs* (New York: Simon & Schuster, 2011), 123.

20. "Drowning Facts," *Centers for Disease Control and Prevention*, May 16, 2024, https://www.cdc.gov/drowning/data-research/facts/index.html.

21. "Drowning," *World Health Organization*, December 13, 2024, https://www.who.int/news-room/fact-sheets/detail/drowning.

22. Sanghamitra Pati et al. "Historic First Global Status Report on Drowning Prevention Highlights Challenges and Opportunities for Preventing Drowning Among Children and Adolescents," *Journal of Paediatrics and Child Health*, April 11, 2025, https://pmc.ncbi.nlm.nih.gov/articles/PMC12053230/.

23. Rin-Rin Yu. "Multiple Drownings Rock Waterpark Industry," *Aquatics International*, September 1, 2007, https://www.aquaticsintl.com/facilities/waterparks-resorts/multiple-drownings-rock-waterpark-industry_0.

24. Dan Martell. *Buy Back Your Time: Get Unstuck, Reclaim Your Freedom, and Build Your Empire* (New York: Portfolio/Penguin, 2023).

25. Dan Martell. *Buy Back Your Time*.

26. This American Life. "NUMMI (2015)," episode 561, July 17, 2015, https://www.thisamericanlife.org/561/nummi-2015.

27. Frank Langfitt. "The End of the Line for GM-Toyota Joint Venture," All Things Considered (*NPR*), March 26, 2010, https://www.npr.org/2010/03/26/125229157/the-end-of-the-line-for-gm-toyota-joint-venture.

28. Brandon Dawson. "How 97% of Businesses Get Stuck Under $3 Million," YouTube video, 0:26, December 14, 2014, https://www.youtube.com/watch?v=Sx27GYb9USo.

29. Michael Gerber. "Systems permit ordinary people to achieve extraordinary results predictably," as attributed in various online sources including QuoteFancy, A-ZQuotes, and LinkedIn, accessed August 6, 2025.

30. U.S. Navy. "Navy SEAL," accessed July 24, 2025, https://www.navy.com/careers-benefits/careers/special-operations/navy-seal.

31. Jeff Bezos. "2016 Letter to Shareholders," *Amazon Company News*, April 17, 2017, https://www.aboutamazon.com/news/company-news/2016-letter-to-shareholders.

32. Russ Britt. "Disney, Pixar agree to $7.4 billion deal," *MarketWatch*, January 24, 2006, https://www.marketwatch.com/story/disney-pixar-agree-to-74-billion-deal.

33. Bob Iger. *The Ride of a Lifetime: Lessons Learned from 15 Years as CEO of the Walt Disney Company* (New York: Crown Publishing Group, 2019).

34. John Lasseter, quoted in "John Lasseter Quotes," IMDb, accessed August 5, 2025, https://www.imdb.com/name/nm0005124/quotes/.

35. Bob Harig. "Officials to keep close eye, ear on fan behavior at Masters," ESPN, April 4, 2018, https://www.espn.com/golf/story/_/id/23029309/augusta-national-officials-keep-close-eye-ear-fan-behavior-masters.

36. Anton Gunn and 937 Strategy Group. "The State of Workplace Injustice 2024 Report," 937 Strategy Group, 2024. https://937strategygroup.com/workplace-injustice-report/.

37. Justin Goodbread. "Building A Company Culture To Drive Success," *Forbes*, September 14, 2023, https://www.forbes.com/councils/forbesfinancecouncil/2023/09/14/building-a-company-culture-to-drive-success/.

38. WM Phoenix Open Sustainability Committee. 2024 *WM Phoenix Open Sustainability Report* (Scottsdale, AZ: Waste Management/PGA Tour, February 2024), PDF. https://www.wm.com/content/dam/wm/assets/inside-wm/phoenix-open/2024-WMPO-Sustainability-Report.pdf.

39. Erik Matuszewski. "Why Augusta National Is Investing in Municipal Golf and 'The Patch,'" *Forbes*, April 11, 2024, https://www.forbes.com/sites/erikmatuszewski/2024/04/11/why-augusta-national-is-investing-in-municipal-golf-and-the-patch/.

40. Jocko Willink and Leif Babin. *Extreme Ownership: How U.S. Navy SEALs Lead and Win* (New York: St. Martin's Press, 2015).

41. Willink. *Extreme Ownership*.

42. Willink. *Extreme Ownership*.

43. "Powering Innovation and Speed with Amazon's Two-Pizza Teams," *AWS Executive Insights*, https://aws.amazon.com/executive-insights/content/amazon-two-pizza-team/.

44. James Anderson. "Denver City Hall Takes a Page From NASA," *Bloomberg*, July 7, 2025, https://www.bloomberg.com/news/articles/2025-07-07/denver-city-hall-takes-a-page-from-nasa-to-tackle-housing-barriers.

45. Andy Grove. *High Output Management* (New York: Vintage Books, 1983), chap. 2.

46. Lou Adler. *The Essential Guide for Hiring & Getting Hired* (Irvine, CA: Adler Group, 2013).

47. Kate Reilly. "Exclusive: How Airbnb Gave Its Candidate Experience a Makeover," *LinkedIn Talent Blog*, March 27, 2014, https://www.

linkedin.com/business/talent/blog/talent-acquisition/airbnb-candidate-experience-makeover.

48. Courtney Connley. "Patriots coach Bill Belichick lives by this brilliant quote from 'The Art of War'," CNBC, January 31, 2019, https://www.cnbc.com/2019/01/31/bill-belichick-uses-this-sun-tzu-quote-to-inspire-the-patriots-to-win.html.

49. Sun Tzu. *The Art of War*, trans. Lionel Giles (New York: Barnes & Noble Classics, 2003), 15. Paraphrased from Chapter 4: Tactical Dispositions.

50. James Clear. "Seinfeld Strategy: How to Stop Procrastinating," *James Clear*, accessed July 24, 2025, https://jamesclear.com/stop-procrastinating-seinfeld-strategy.

51. Joydeep Singh. "'I Hit Thousands of Balls, Hands Bleeding, Aching, Just So That I Could Play...': Tiger Woods Recalled His Dad's Powerful Advice at His HOF Ceremony," *EssentiallySports*, June 27, 2022, https://www.essentiallysports.com/golf-news-i-hit-thousands-of-balls-hands-bleeding-aching-just-so-that-i-could-play-tiger-woods-recalled-his-dads-powerful-advice-at-his-hof-ceremony/.

52. KISSmetrics. "Calculating Lifetime Value (LTV): A Case Study – Starbucks," PDF, August 2011, https://blog.kissmetrics.com/wp-content/uploads/2011/08/calculating-ltv.pdf.

53. Ben Ryder Howe. "How Costco Hacked the American Shopping Psyche," *The New York Times*, August 20, 2024, https://www.nytimes.com/2024/08/20/dining/costco.html.

54. Sam Walton. "If you don't listen to your customers, someone else will," as attributed in various online sources including QuoteFancy, A-ZQuotes, and Quartr, accessed August 5, 2025.

55. Jesse Itzler. "26.2 MILES OF FREE ADVERTISING," Instagram, November 4, 2023, https://www.instagram.com/p/CzOr3wSAOob/?hl=en.

56. Itzler. "26.2 MILES OF FREE ADVERTISING."

57. Peter Economy. "17 Zig Ziglar Quotes That Will Inspire You to Achieve More and Be More," *Inc. Magazine*, November 9, 2024, https://www.inc.com/peter-economy/17-zig-ziglar-quotes-that-will-inspire-you-to-achieve-more-and-be-more/90992629.

58. Eddie Yoon, Steve Carlotti, Dennis Moore. "Make Your Best Customers Even Better," *Harvard Business Review*, March, 2014, https://hbr.org/2014/03/make-your-best-customers-even-better.

59. Cat Symonds. "The rule of 7: The power of social media," Factorial, April 9, 2025, https://factorialhr.com/blog/the-rule-of-7/.

60. Yvon Chouinard, interview by Guy Raz. "How I Built This," *NPR*, December 25, 2017, podcast audio, https://www.npr.org/2018/02/06/572558864/patagonia-yvon-chouinard.

61. Alex Hormozi. "If I Opened a Sandwich Shop…," Facebook, July 13, 2024, https://www.facebook.com/watch/?v=1927638367750967.

62. Chip Wilson, interview by Tim Ferriss. The Tim Ferriss Show, May 19, 2021, podcast audio, https://tim.blog/2021/05/19/chip-wilson/.

63. Bo Burlingham. "Patagonia's 100-Year Plan: Yvon Chouinard to Elevate Social Mission," *Inc. Magazine*, July 10, 2014, https://www.inc.com/magazine/201407/bo-burlingham/yvon-chouinards-business-plan-prioritizes-social-mission.html.

64. Yvon Chouinard. "How This $700 Million Business Makes Money Without Trying to Turn a Profit," *Inc. Magazine*, September 26, 2016, https://www.inc.com/yvon-chouinard/patagonia-ceo-let-my-people-go-surfing-why-company-mission-is-not-profit.html.

65. Warren Buffett. "Price is what you pay. Value is what you get," as attributed in various online sources including GoodReads, A-ZQuotes, and BrainyQuote, accessed August 5, 2025.

66. Shep Hyken. "Ninety-Six Percent Of Customers Will Leave You For Bad Customer Service," *Forbes*, July 12, 2020, https://www.forbes.com/sites/shephyken/2020/07/12/ninety-six-percent-of-customers-will-leave-you-for-bad-customer-service/.

67. Amelia Lucas. "Every restaurant wants to beat Chick-fil-A, but it's stronger than ever," *CNBC*, December 21, 2023, https://www.cnbc.com/2023/12/21/chick-fil-a-stronger-than-ever-amid-more-competition.html.

68. Chip Wilson, The Tim Ferriss Show.

69. Ryan Holiday. "All You Need Are a Few Small Wins Every Day," RyanHoliday.net, https://ryanholiday.net/all-you-need-are-a-few-small-wins-every-day/.

70.  Holy Bible, King James Version, Prov. 13:20.

71.  Nicholas A. Christakis and James H. Fowler. "The Spread of Obesity in a Large Social Network over 32 Years," *New England Journal of Medicine* 357, no. 4 (2007): 370-79, https://doi.org/10.1056/NEJMsa066082.

72.  Clive Thompson. "Are Your Friends Making You Fat?," *The New York Times Magazine*, September 10, 2009, https://www.nytimes.com/2009/09/13/magazine/13contagion-t.html.

73.  David Burkus. "You're NOT The Average Of The Five People You Surround Yourself With," Medium.com, May 23, 2018, https://medium.com/the-mission/youre-not-the-average-of-the-five-people-you-surround-yourself-with-f21b817f6e69.

74.  Nicholas A. Christakis and James H. Fowler. "The Collective Dynamics of Smoking in a Large Social Network," *New England Journal of Medicine* 358, no. 21 (2008), https://www.nejm.org/doi/full/10.1056/NEJMsa0706154.

75.  Rose McDermott, James H. Fowler, and Nicholas A. Christakis. "Breaking Up Is Hard to Do, Unless Everyone Else Is Doing It Too: Social Network Effects on Divorce in a Longitudinal Sample," SSRN Scholarly Paper (Rochester, NY: *Social Science Research Network*, October 18, 2009), accessed August 8, 2025, https://papers.ssrn.com/abstract=1490708.

76.  Dylan Minor and Michael Housman. "Sitting Near a High-Performer Can Make You Better at Your Job," *Kellogg Insight*, Northwestern University, May 8, 2017, https://insight.kellogg.

northwestern.edu/article/sitting-near-a-high-performer-can-make-you-better-at-your-job.

77. Mark Hyman. "Community is medicine," Facebook, April 29, 2025, https://www.facebook.com/drmarkhyman/posts/pfbid02fWJN3X1YEaz7cqbgXUCJ3uWqDDjgnZECBjX2Q2uTCwTLzjVEQEkEjNTZgZHJoikGl.

78. Climbing Kilimanjaro. "How Many People Climb Mount Everest?," accessed August 6, 2025, https://www.climbing-kilimanjaro.com/how-many-people-climb-mount-everest/.

79. "Jordan Romero, 13, 'becomes youngest to scale Everest'," *BBC News*, May 22, 2010, https://www.bbc.com/news/10141547.

80. "Japanese 80-year-old claims Everest Record," *BBC News*, May 23, 2013, https://www.bbc.com/news/world-asia-22634683.

81. "Double amputee Xia Boyu makes history on Everest Summit," *BBC News*, May 14, 2018, https://www.bbc.com/news/world-asia-44112710.

82. Clay Skipper. "From Productivity to Psychedelics: Tim Ferriss Has Changed His Mind About Success," *GQ*, July 22, 2020, https://www.gq.com/story/tim-ferriss-interview-quarantine-psychedelics.

83. Mary Ellen Biery. "Study Shows Why Many Business Owners Can't Sell When They Want To," *Forbes*, February 5, 2017, https://www.forbes.com/sites/sageworks/2017/02/05/these-8-stats-show-why-many-business-owners-cant-sell-when-they-want-to/.

84. Michael Cohn. "Bad financial reporting estimated to cost billions," *Accounting Today*, January 13, 2022, https://www.accountingtoday.com/news/bad-financial-reporting-estimated-to-cost-companies-billions.

# ABOUT THE AUTHOR

Cameron Bawden is a serial entrepreneur, mentor, and creator dedicated to helping service-based business owners scale smarter, lead better, and improve 1% every single day—both personally and professionally.

Cameron has built, scaled, and sold multiple companies, including Arizona's largest privately owned pest control company, Green Mango Pest Control.

Having achieved more than $100 million in total exits across several ventures, Bawden now mentors other ambitious owners inside *The 1% Club*. He lives in Arizona with his wife and two children.

For more information about Cameron's 1% Club, scan the QR code below:

# ABOUT THE PUBLISHER

Legacy Launch Pad is a boutique publishing company that works with entrepreneurs from all over the world.

For more information about Legacy Launch Pad Publishing, go to: www.legacylaunchpadpub.com.